T0119093

Tucson
Hiking Guide

Tucson Hiking Guide

FOURTH EDITION

BETTY LEAVENGOOD

WestWinds Press®

P R U E T T
The Pruett Series

© 1991, 1996, 2004, 2012 by Betty Leavengood

All rights reserved. No part of this book may be reproduced without written permission from the publisher, except in the case of brief excerpts in critical reviews and articles.

Fourth Edition

Library of Congress Cataloging-in-Publication Data

Leavengood, Betty, 1939-
    Tucson hiking guide / Betty Leavengood. — 4th ed.
       p. cm.
    Originally published: Boulder : Pruett Publishing, c1992.
    Includes bibliographical references and index.
    ISBN 978-0-87108-966-3 (pbk.)
    1. Hiking—Arizona—Tucson Region—Guidebooks 2. Hiking—
Arizona—Tucson Region—Safety measures. 3. Tuscon Region
(Ariz.)—Guidebooks. I. Title.
GV199.42.A72T835 2013
796.5109791'776—dc23
                    2012047262

West Winds Press®
An imprint of Turner Publishing Company
4507 Charlotte Avenue, Suite 100
Nashville, TN 37209
(615) 255-2665
www.turnerbookstore.com

Interior design and composition by Dianne Nelson, Shadow Canyon Graphics. Front cover caption: Bret Paulk enjoys hiking the Agua Caliente Hill Trail in the Santa Catalina Mountains. Cover photo by Wendy Davis.

CONTENTS

Preface vii
Introduction 1
Getting Ready 4
Hazards of Hiking Around Tucson 6
Trail Difficulty Ratings 13

THE TUCSON MOUNTAINS **15**
    Hugh Norris Trail 18
    King Canyon Trail 24
    Ez-Kim-In-Zin Picnic Area to Signal Hill 29
    Sendero Esperanza Trail 34
    Sweetwater Trail 39
    Roadrunner–Panther Peak Wash–Cam-Boh Trail Loop 44
    David Yetman Trail 50
    Brown Mountain Trail 55
    Cam-Boh–Ironwood Forest–Picture Rocks Wash–
        Ringtail Loop .... .60

THE RINCON MOUNTAINS **65**
    Cactus Forest Trail 68
    Broadway Trailhead to Garwood Dam .... .73
    Tanque Verde Ridge Trail 78
    Douglas Spring Trail 84
    Rincon Peak Trail 90
    Quilter Trail 96

Contents

THE SANTA CATALINA MOUNTAINS **101**
    Agua Caliente Hill Trail 103
    Bug Spring Trail 108
    Mount Lemmon to Catalina State Park 113
    Blackett's Ridge Trail 119
    Esperero Trail 124
    Ventana Canyon Trail 130
    Pontatoc Ridge Trail 136
    Finger Rock Trail 141
    Pima Canyon Trail 147
    Box Camp Trail 153
    Romero Canyon Trail 159
    Hirabayashi Recreation Site to Sabino Canyon 164
    Hutch's Pool 170

THE SANTA RITA MOUNTAINS **175**
    Old Baldy Trail 177
    Super Trail 184
    Kent Spring–Bog Springs Loop Trail 190
    Dutch John Spring Trail 195
    Agua Caliente (Vault Mine)–Josephine Saddle
        Loop Trail 199
    Elephant Head Trail 204
    Arizona Trail: From Kentucky Camp to
        Gardner Canyon Road 209
    Tunnel Spring Loop Trail 215

Selected Readings 221
About the Author 222
Index 223

PREFACE

When the *Tucson Hiking Guide* was first published in the spring of 1991, I did not realize that it would become a lifetime work! This is the fourth edition. Again, as in previous editions, new trails have been added, existing trails have been rerouted, and government fees and regulations have changed.

Although there are many changes, this edition remains a guide for the "Sunday hiker." Years ago, my parents and I would often go for a Sunday drive. We'd stop on a whim, walk around the lake, visit a relative, or get an ice cream cone at the Dairy Queen. So it is with Sunday hikers. They start up the trail at a leisurely pace, stopping on a whim to inspect a pack rat's nest or take in the view. Maybe they come upon an old foundation and wonder who built it, or they may ask, "Why is this trail named Pontatoc?"

If you are a Sunday hiker, this is the guide for you. You'll find detailed instructions to the trailhead from the intersection of Speedway Boulevard and Campbell Avenue. Once on the trail, you'll find the directions are specific. I, never having been too familiar with a compass, say turn "left or right" instead of "east or west." If possible, I include the history of the trail. If there's an old house, as on the David Yetman Trail, I'll tell you why it's there.

In this fourth edition, I've been helped by many people. My daughters, Cheryl and Christine Graham, each assisted with the fourth edition. Cheryl turned my rough sketches into understandable trail profiles. Christine hiked several trails with me including the David Yetman, Ventana Canyon, Pontatoc Canyon, and Broadway Trailhead to Garwood Dam Trails. Chris Zalewski, Jo Haslett, Rebecca McCaleb, and I trekked down the newly opened Bug Spring Trail. Chris also went with me to double-check the route to Elephant Head. Carolyn O'Bagy Davis helped me identify the ironwood trees on the Cam-Boh-Ironwood Forest-Picture Rocks Wash-Ringtail Loop in the Tucson Mountains.

Lisa Foster, Jim Bowen, and I hiked several of the most challenging trails: the Box Camp Trail which begins near Milepost 22 on the Catalina Highway and ends in Sabino Canyon; the Mount Lemmon Trail which, in combination with the Romero Trail, goes from the summit of Mount Lemmon to Catalina State Park; the Tunnel Spring Loop Trail in the Santa Rita Mountains that includes the Ditch and Walker Basin Trails; nearly to the top of Rincon Peak for an overnighter at Happy Valley Campground; and the newly opened Quilter Trail.

INTRODUCTION

Tucson is a "hiker's heaven." To the north is the mountain range that dominates the Tucson skyline, the Santa Catalina range. Due east are the Rincons. Forty miles south of town are the Santa Rita Mountains. The Tucson Mountains to the west are the backdrop for our dramatic sunsets. Hiking is possible year-round—the mild winters allow hiking in the lower elevations, and, in summer, the trails of the high mountains beckon.

To enjoy hiking in these mountains, you must be properly prepared and be aware of the hazards of hiking in this area. Too much exposure to the sun is dangerous. Not carrying enough water can result in serious illness or death. There are venomous creatures out there, such as rattlesnakes, scorpions, and Gila monsters. Cactus, amole, catclaw, and other thorny plants seem determined to attack you. Weather conditions can change quickly—what started out as a beautiful morning can become a storm by early afternoon.

Sounds bad! If you are properly prepared and aware of the dangers that exist, the chances of anything happening to you are remote. It is beautiful out there, and the only way you can see it is on your feet. Within a forty-five-mile radius of Tucson, the elevations go from 2,500 feet to nearly 10,000 feet. Vegetation changes from cactus to oak to ponderosa pine and Douglas fir. You may spot a javelina, coyote, deer, or in the highest elevations, even a bear. Hidden pools invite swimming on a hot day. The views extend seemingly forever or are limited by stark canyon walls.

This guide is intended to prepare you to hike in these mountains. The first chapter will discuss proper equipment and clothing for hiking here. The second chapter discusses what you should be aware of, such as too much sun, too little water, and those poisonous creatures. The rest of the guide is devoted to providing detailed descriptions of trails and is organized by mountain range.

Each hike is preceded by a box of information as follows:

General Description: A short description of the hike.

Difficulty: I used four categories—"easy" is a hike with minimum elevation gain or loss that nearly anyone could achieve; "moderate" is a little harder, usually over 1,000 feet in elevation gain and over three miles one way; "difficult" has areas of steep elevation gain and will require most of the day; "extremely difficult" is a category that is limited to a few hikes in this guide. They require a long day, are usually over five miles one way, and are steep.

Best Time of Year to Hike: Exactly what it says.

Length: Distance given is round-trip, unless it is a loop hike, then the distance refers to the entire loop.

Miles to Trailhead from Speedway/Campbell Intersection: This is a major well-known intersection in Tucson.

Directions to Trailhead from Speedway/Campbell Intersection: Specific directions are given from this intersection and can be adapted from any place in town. All hikes in this guide are on trails and all can be reached by passenger car.

Fees: Many of the trails are in fee areas. It is noted in the trail description if a pass is required to hike that particular trail. Passes are available as follows: Coronado Recreation Pass (Daily $5, Weekly $10, Annual $20) and America the Beautiful series, which includes Annual Pass ($80), Senior Pass ($10 Lifetime Pass), Access Pass (Free Lifetime Pass for permanently disabled US Citizens, and Volunteer Pass (Annual Pass awarded to volunteers who contribute 250 hours of more). All passes are available at the Coronado National Forest office at 300 W. Congress Street in Tucson, the Sabino Canyon Visitor Center, and Saguaro National Park—East and West. The Coronado Recreation Pass may also be purchased at the Santa Rita Lodge in Madera Canyon.

Although I have made every effort to ensure the accuracy of the directions, you must take the final responsibility for translating that information to your vehicle and hiking boots. A government agency may change a trailhead or a street name. Heavy rains can wash out a section of a trail, or what appears to me as a distinctive landmark may mean nothing to you. Always carry this guide, a map of the area you are hiking, a compass, and a cell phone. Never, never hike alone. Do not overestimate your hiking ability and do not hesitate to turn back if you become disoriented. It is better to try again another day than to become the subject of a story on the evening news!

GETTING READY

Shoes. Most of the trails in the Tucson area are rocky and steep, making a sturdy hiking boot with ankle support a must. Many styles are available from all-leather to a combination of leather and fabric. Without comfortable boots, hiking can be extremely unpleasant.

Socks. Wear two pairs—a thin inner pair and an outer pair of wool or wool/cotton blend.

Clothing. Wear layers. A cotton T-shirt, a lightweight long-sleeved cotton shirt, and a sweater or sweatshirt are good to start with. Lightweight long pants protect your legs from the thorny vegetation. Many hikes in this area start at a low elevation and climb several thousand feet, requiring more clothing at the top than at the beginning of the hike. Layering makes it possible to be comfortable at any elevation.

Hat. Wear a hat for protection from the sun. Many styles are available. I prefer a cotton hat with a wide brim that can be tossed in the washer after a few wearings.

Walking Stick. In the rough terrain around Tucson, a walking stick is helpful. Many styles are available for purchase, or you can make one of your own. I have seen several strong sticks made out of agave stalks, with rubber tips on the ends to prevent splitting.

Daypack. Many styles are available. I prefer a daypack with several pockets large enough to hold some permanent supplies. Keep a first aid kit, knife, compass, lightweight poncho, sunscreen, aspirin, and insect repellent tucked away in one pocket of the daypack. There should be room for extra bottles of water, plenty of food, and a warm jacket.

Canteen. Many types of canteens are available. Whatever style you select, make sure that it is easy to get at while you're hiking. I prefer a bottle holder that fits a belt. You'll need extra water bottles to carry in your daypack. You can also purchase all sizes and shapes of water bottles at outdoor stores.

Map. Although there are individual trail maps included in this guide, an overall map of the mountain range is helpful. United States Geological Survey Maps are available for each range.

Cell Phone. The number of rescues by the local search and rescue organization have been greatly reduced by hikers carrying cell phones. Often a rescue is initiated when the missing hiker is just late. By having a cell phone, the rescue is avoided by a call. Also in case of an emergency, a cell phone can be used to seek help.

HAZARDS OF HIKING AROUND TUCSON

Hiking in the mountains around Tucson presents a hiker with several unique situations. The sun is intense; water is scarce; venomous creatures abound; the newly discovered hantavirus strikes victims quickly; Africanized "killer" bees are aggressive when disturbed; lightning strikes here are higher than in any other place in the United States, with the exception of an area near Naples, Florida; and, yes, it is totally possible to get hypothermia while hiking in the desert.

Sun. The sun shines here 360 days a year, according to the Chamber of Commerce. It's great for hiking and not so great for the skin.

The University of Arizona Cancer Center sponsors the Skin Cancer Institute to make Tucsonans aware of the dangers of too much exposure to the sun. Skin cancer is caused by the ultraviolet rays of the sun. Many geographic and meteorologic factors in southern Arizona combine to allow high intensities of ultraviolet radiation to reach the earth's surface. These factors include Tucson's 32 degree north latitude, 2,410-foot altitude, high number of clear days, high annual percentage of sunlight, and a high average daily temperature that encourages outdoor activity. The Tucson *Arizona Daily Star* publishes the ultraviolet index (UVI) daily. At a higher altitude the UVI numbers increase.

Despite the danger of skin cancer, it is possible to hike safely in the sun. The cardinal rule to remember is never hike in the Tucson area without a sunscreen that has a sun protection factor (SPF) of at least 15. Sunscreens block the ultraviolet rays. The ratings, which are given for untanned Caucasians, assume there are no clouds and indicate the number of minutes of exposure to the sun required to redden the skin

6

at various times during the day. The intensity varies from sixteen minutes at noon in the summer to thirty minutes at noon during the winter months. For example, if you plan to be in the sun in July at noon, it would only take sixteen minutes for your skin to redden. A sunscreen with an SPF of 15 would lengthen the time that you could safely be exposed to the sun. A good formula to use is the "times ten" rule. For instance, an SPF of 15 will protect for 150 minutes (15 times 10), 2.5 hours.

Many sunscreens are available. A few have an SPF as high as 100. Several are water resistant. Follow the instructions for use that are on the product, which basically include applying the sunscreen thirty minutes before exposure and reapplying it after swimming or heavy perspiration. Experiment and see which product suits your skin best. Today's sunscreens are like fine lotions and have no medicinal odor.

In addition to sunscreen, the hiker should wear a wide-brimmed hat, a long-sleeved cotton shirt, and lightweight long pants. Sunglasses that screen ultraviolet rays are a necessity. It is best, although usually not practical when hiking, to avoid exposure to the sun between 10 A.M. and 3 P.M. In the summer, hiking should be confined to the higher elevations, because of the intensity of the sun and the extreme heat at lower levels.

Water. Water is so important in Arizona that many statutes regulate its consumption and use. Each summer newspapers carry accounts of death and near death from lack of water. At the least, too little water can cause headache, nausea, cramps, and fatigue. Although water consumption is especially important in summer, because of the low humidity, adequate intake is important in all seasons.

Kevin Kregel, professor of Exercise Science at the University of Iowa, researched the effects of heat stress on the thermoregulatory and cardiovascular responses, or, in layman's terms, "what happens if you don't get enough to drink."

Kregel recommends that hikers pre-hydrate by drinking twenty ounces of fluid two hours before hiking. During the hike, they should take a good drink every fifteen minutes. Kregel warns, "By the time you feel thirsty, you are already slightly dehydrated." For hikes of long duration, Kregel recommends drinking a fluid-replacement beverage such as Gatorade. Avoid soda pop, fruit juices, caffeinated drinks, and alcoholic beverages—all act as diuretics and cause dehydration.

One bit of good news! The idea that hikers shouldn't drink cold water is no longer accepted. According to Kregel, current research shows that cold water is absorbed into the body quicker. In fact, Kregel recommends what I have been doing for years—"Freeze it!"

Venomous Creatures. Venomous creatures—snakes, scorpions, and Gila monsters—are prevalent in the Sonoran Desert and mountains around Tucson.

Arizona reportedly has more rattlesnakes than any other state. Regardless of who's counting, Arizona rattlers have the best press agent! Rarely is there a Western made without a coiled rattler in the center of the trail. The horse rears, our hero pulls his gun and shoots the snake between the eyes, thus averting certain disaster. In reality, rattlers present little threat to riders or hikers.

True, rattlers thrive in the canyons and mountains around Tucson. Of the eleven species of rattlers, the western diamondback is the most common, and the one you are most likely to see while hiking. The western diamondback is brownish-gray with diamond-shaped markings. It has a broad triangular head, and at the end of its tail is a "rattle"—a series of connected bony segments, which, when vibrated, make a sound similar to a baby's rattle.

The Arizona Poison and Drug Information Center receives many calls a year regarding rattlesnake bites in Arizona. The majority of bites are "illegitimate"—that is, incurred while someone, usually a fifteen- to twenty-five-year-old male, is playing with the snake. Many of these bites happen when people are drinking, leading the staff of the Poison Control Center to say "snakes are attracted to alcohol!" "Legitimate" bites, those suffered accidentally, are rare, although their number has increased in recent years.

While hiking, observe a few simple precautions. Since most bites happen to the extremities, do not put your hands or feet under a rock or log or anyplace else a snake might be sleeping. Never sit down without looking. Wear sturdy hiking boots that cannot be penetrated by fangs and long pants that will hinder the effect of a bite. If you see a snake, assume that it is poisonous and give it a wide berth. If you hear a rattle, stop immediately, determine the location of the snake, and get away from it.

If you or someone in your hiking party should be bitten, the single most important thing you can do is to remain calm and seek medical care.

Some specialists are beginning to cautiously recommend use of Sawyer Venom Extractor, an inexpensive device that uses a vacuum suction to extract venom. The kit must be used immediately after the bite occurs and the cup that catches the blood must be continuously emptied. The Arizona Poison and Drug Information Center is not yet officially recommending the use of the kit until more studies have been conducted.

The center does recommend applying a wide constricting band between the bite and the heart, making sure that the band is loose enough so that a finger can be inserted between it and the limb. Complications can occur with an improperly applied band. Also, if possible, immobilize the limb with a splint or a sling.

Until recently, experts recommended cutting across the bite and sucking the venom out. More damage can be caused by the cut than by the actual bite. Other don'ts include: don't apply ice to the bite area; don't give the victim alcohol; and don't waste time catching the snake, because today's antivenins are effective against the bites of all pit vipers, regardless of their kind.

Scorpions also unnecessarily strike fear into the hearts of hikers. Of the thirty species of scorpions in Arizona, only one, the bark scorpion, is poisonous. Although chances of a fatality from a scorpion bite are remote (no deaths have occurred in Arizona in thirty years), caution should nevertheless be observed. Scorpions spend the daylight hours under cover and only emerge at night, and then, only when the nighttime lows exceed 77 degrees Fahrenheit. The bark scorpion never burrows and is most commonly found in riparian areas, such as in desert canyons and in groves of mesquite, cottonwood, and Arizona sycamore. The bark scorpion is most likely to bite when disturbed by a hiker leaning on a tree or moving a log. Although the bark scorpion can be distinguished from other species, any scorpion bite should be taken seriously. If possible, capture the scorpion so it can be determined if it is a bark scorpion.

The best first-aid treatment for a scorpion bite is to get to a medical facility as soon as possible. If you cannot reach medical assistance, apply a loose constricting band between the sting and the heart.

The Gila monster also has a good press agent. The Gila monster is a brilliantly colored black and yellow or black and pink creature, so rare that it is protected by Arizona state law. Legend has it that once a Gila monster bites, it will not release its victim until thunder is heard. Although Gila monsters are the only lizard in the United States whose bite is poisonous, danger to hikers from Gila monsters is negligible. They are rarely seen in the wild. If one is seen at all, it will most likely be at dusk or after a summer rain in a canyon bottom, where the lizard has access to moist soil. To get bitten by a Gila monster while hiking, you would practically have to fall near one and surprise it. The overwhelming majority of bites have occurred to people handling captive Gila monsters.

Should you or a member of your party get bitten by a Gila monster, you don't have to wait until it thunders. A Gila monster will, however, hold on for at least fifteen minutes, during which time venom is pouring into the wound. The first thing to do is to get the Gila monster to release its grasp so as to limit the amount of venom that is injected into the body. A strong stick between the jaws usually works. If the stick is ineffective, the Gila monster may be encouraged to release its grip if you place an open flame under its jaw. Immersing the wounded extremity and the Gila monster under water might also work. If neither a stick, flame, nor water is available, grab the Gila monster by the tail and jerk. This will cause more damage to the wound, but anything is better than letting the Gila monster retain its grip.

First aid for a Gila monster bite involves letting the wound bleed freely for several minutes, while you flush it with water. Apply a loose constricting band between the wound and the heart. Immobilize the limb and seek medical help as soon as possible.

Further information and advice is available twenty-four hours a day from the Arizona Poison and Drug Information Center. In Tucson call 1-800-362-0101.

Hantavirus. This recently discovered deadly disease is thought to be transmitted when humans inhale particles of dried rodent urine and feces. Hikers should avoid contact with rodent-infested structures, such as abandoned cabins. All food should be carried in rodent-proof containers, and care should be taken to avoid rodent burrows.

Lightning. Lightning can be deadly in the mountains surrounding the city. Summer monsoon storms come up quickly and you need to take precautions when they do. Get off peaks, cliffs, and the ends of ridges. If you are in the forest, try to find a clump of trees shorter than the surrounding trees. Toss anything metal, such as a drinking cup or metal hiking stick, far away from you. If you are caught out in the open, squat on the ground and rest your head on your knees. Do not lie on the ground or get in a drainage ditch. Deep caves are safe, but stay away from shallow rock overhangs. Finally, if you are in a group, keep at least 50 feet apart to reduce the chance of everyone being struck. If someone in your party is struck by lightning, immediately begin CPR and seek medical assistance.

Hypothermia. Hypothermia, the lowering of the body's core temperature, is generally thought of as a condition that occurs in higher elevations than exist around Tucson. However, sudden changes in weather conditions here, especially atop the mountain ranges, can bring on cold rain or snow and cause the body temperature to fall to dangerous levels. Symptoms of hypothermia include drowsiness, uncontrollable shivering, impaired judgment, and weakness. Often victims do not realize that they are developing hypothermia, thus, it is always best to hike with a companion. The best treatment for hypothermia is to avoid it in the first place. Layer clothing and always keep rain gear, such as an inexpensive, lightweight poncho, in your daypack. Carry extra high-energy bars and always drink plenty of liquid. Should someone in your party develop hypothermia, immediately replace wet clothing with dry. Huddle with the person to help transfer warmth to their body, give warm liquids if possible, and seek medical assistance as soon as possible. Hypothermia can be deadly.

Africanized Bees. African bees were brought to South America to help increase honey production. In 1957 these bees began moving north, reaching Arizona in 1993. They are nicknamed "killer bees" because they are far more aggressive than other bees. Humans and animals have died in Arizona from Africanized bee attacks. The Arizona Department of Agriculture Africanized Honey Bee Advisory Committee advises wearing light-colored clothing while hiking and avoiding all scented products. If attacked, run as far and as fast as possible, preferably into brush. If you are stung, seek medical attention.

All this sounds formidable. Don't let it deter you from hiking and enjoying the out-of-doors. Just be aware of the dangers that exist and be prepared for emergencies.

TRAIL
DIFFICULTY
RATINGS

What follows is a totally unscientific rating of the trails in this guide, dividing them into four categories: Extremely Difficult trails are long, steep, tortuous climbs into the high country that should be attempted only by experienced hikers. Difficult trails are fairly long, but occasionally short and very steep, which, although difficult, don't have that built-in torture factor characteristic of the extremely difficult category. Moderate trails are pleasant hikes with some climbing, but not enough to really strain your muscles. Easy trails are rambles that nearly anyone can do.

EXTREMELY DIFFICULT

Trail	Mountain Range	Page
Rincon Peak Trail	Rincon Mts.	90
Esperero Trail	Santa Catalina Mts.	124
Mt. Lemmon/Catalina Park	Santa Catalina Mts.	113
Finger Rock Trail	Santa Catalina Mts.	141
Box Camp Trail	Santa Catalina Mts.	153
Old Baldy Trail	Santa Rita Mts.	177
Elephant Head Trail	Santa Rita Mts.	204

DIFFICULT

Trail	Mountain Range	Page
Tanque Verde Ridge Trail	Rincon Mts.	78
Douglas Spring Trail	Rincon Mts.	84
Pima Canyon Trail	Santa Catalina Mts.	147
Agua Caliente Hill Trail	Santa Catalina Mts.	103

Ventana Canyon Trail	Santa Catalina Mts.	130
Bug Spring Trail	Santa Catalina Mts.	108
Super Trail	Santa Rita Mts.	184
Agua Caliente–J Saddle Loop	Santa Rita Mts.	199
Tunnel Spring Loop	Santa Rita Mts.	215
Quilter Trail	Rincon Mts.	96
Hugh Norris Trail	Tucson Mts.	18
Sweetwater Trail	Tucson Mts.	39

MODERATE

Trail	Mountain Range	Page
King Canyon Trail	Tucson Mts.	24
Sendero Esperanza Trail	Tucson Mts	34
David Yetman Trail	Tucson Mts.	50
Brown Mountain Trail	Tucson Mts.	55
Broadway Trailhead to Garwood Dam	Rincon Mts.	73
Blackett's Ridge Trail	Santa Catalina Mts.	119
Hirabayashi to Sabino Canyon	Santa Catalina Mts.	164
Hutch's Pool	Santa Catalina Mts.	170
Pontatoc Ridge Trail	Santa Catalina Mts.	136
Romero Canyon Trail	Santa Catalina Mts.	159
Kent/Bog Springs	Santa Rita Mts.	190
Dutch John Spring Trail	Santa Rita Mts.	195
Arizona Trail— Kentucky Camp to Gardner Canyon	Santa Rita Mts.	209

EASY

Trail	Mountain Range	Page
Cactus Forest Trail	Rincon Mts.	68
Ez-Kim-In-Zin to Signal Hill	Tucson Mts.	29
Cam-Boh-Ringtail Loop	Tucson Mts.	60
Roadrunner-Cam-Boh	Tucson Mts.	44

THE
TUCSON
MOUNTAINS

Tucson's sunsets are one of our city's trademarks. The mountains silhouetted on postcards are the Tucson Mountains, the smallest of the four ranges that surround Tucson. The high point, Wasson Peak at 4,687 feet, is barely a mountain by most standards.

The Tucson Mountains are different in character from the other ranges. No ponderosa pines will shade your path while you are hiking here. This is the land of mesquite and palo verde, of the saguaro, prickly pear, cholla, and hedgehog cacti, of creosote bushes, ocotillo, and cat-claw. The terrain is a jumble of boulders and craggy ridges.

From 300 A.D. to 1500 A.D., the Hohokam lived in the river bottoms in their pit houses and hunted in the Tucson Mountains. Petroglyphs in King Canyon and Picture Rocks remain as evidence of the Hohokam's existence. The Hohokam were gone when Jesuit priest Father Kino first came to the Tucson area in 1692. By then the Pima, now known as the Tohono O'odham, were living at the base of the mountain we now call Sentinel Peak, or "A" Mountain.

The Tucson Mountains were significant in the early history of Tucson. When in 1772, King Carlos III of Spain, who possessed this land on paper, issued an order calling for the reorganization of the presidios (forts) in Mexico and the Southwest, the site selected was a point near the Santa Cruz River opposite the Pima village. Here, beginning in 1776, a new presidio was to be built. Progress was slow, and it was not until December 1783 that the task was completed. A lookout was maintained on top of Sentinel Peak, and the fort was warned when the Apaches swept down out of the Santa Catalinas or the Rincons. Several attacks were withstood, and the Royal Presidio of San Agustin del Tucson outgrew the walls of the fort by the mid-1800s. Sentinel Peak was no longer needed as a lookout.

The mountain did serve other purposes. Many early Tucson homes and the wall around the University of Arizona were built from black rock quarried from the side of Sentinel Peak. Today, a large "A" representing the University of Arizona dominates the peak.

Copper was discovered in the 1870s at Silver Bell, and mining became important. Hikers in the Tucson Mountains today can see much evidence of early mining. The Sendero Esperanza Trail passes the old Gould Mine, once thought to be the bonanza of the territory. The Hugh Norris Trail passes several mines.

As late as the 1920s and 1930s the land in the Tucson Mountains was open to homesteading. A stone house remains on the David Yetman Trail that was homesteaded in 1930 by a newspaperman from Illinois. Ranchers ran cattle in the mountains.

It seemed that the Tucson Mountains were open for grabs. Mining, cattle grazing, and homesteading were being carried on with little regard for the ecology of the mountains, until Pima County agricultural agent C. B. Brown took it upon himself to preserve the Tucson Mountain area. With the help of Senator Carl Hayden, Brown was able to persuade Congress to withdraw 60,000 acres from the Homesteading Act of 1873 to be used as Tucson Mountain Park.

World War I veterans complained that their rights were being violated because they could not homestead, and, as a result, all but 28,988 acres were turned back over to the United States Department of Interior to be used for homesteading. On April 11, 1929, the remaining acreage was designated as Tucson Mountain Park. The Pima County Parks Commission was established, and Brown was named chairman.

In 1933, part of the land designated for homesteading became part of Saguaro National Monument. In 1994, the designation was changed to Saguaro National Park.

The area was still not pristine and secure from development. Mining was still permitted on much of the land. In 1939 Columbia Pictures leased 300 acres of state land that was within the park for movie production and built Old Tucson. In one scene, 6 acres of desert were set on fire, completely destroying all vegetation, including several mature saguaros. Public uproar caused the Pima County Park Commission to purchase the lease from Columbia Pictures, ensuring control and that no fires would be set in the desert again. In 1952, Arthur Pack, a member of the park commission, recommended a living museum be established in Tucson Mountain Park to educate the public about the Sonoran Desert, and the world famous Arizona-Sonora Desert Museum was formed. This excellent facility competes with the Grand Canyon as the most visited attraction in Arizona.

In 1961 President John Kennedy added 15,360 acres of federally owned land in Tucson Mountain Park to the Saguaro National Monument, to be administered by the National Park Service. This change of jurisdiction was made specifically to prevent mining claims in the area and to preserve the natural beauty. Because of this move, the Tucson Mountain Park was reduced to 13,628 acres, to which an additional 3,000 acres were added in 1974, as a result of a bond election.

As you will see in the following descriptions, the trails in the Tucson Mountains are not difficult. Several are rated as "easy." A good introduction to this area is to hike the David Yetman Trail, using a two-car shuttle. The Hugh Norris Trail to the summit of Wasson Peak is the most difficult trail, but the one that provides the best views of the Tucson area. A final note: These mountains are ideal for winter hiking and cool early spring and late fall days. By summer, it is way too hot.

Hugh Norris Trail

General Description: A pleasant ridge ramble past an old mine, to the highest peak in the Tucson Mountains

Difficulty: Difficult, some areas of steep switchbacks

Best Time of Year to Hike: Winter

Length: 9.8 miles round-trip

Miles to Trailhead from Speedway/Campbell Intersection: 19 miles

Directions to Trailhead from Speedway/Campbell Intersection: Go west on Speedway 11.8 miles to the intersection of Kinney Road. (Note: At the intersection of Anklam Road, Speedway becomes Gates Pass Road.) Turn right on Kinney Road, following the signs to Saguaro National Park. The entrance to the park is past the Arizona-Sonora Desert Museum, is signed, and is to the right. Turn into the park and drive past the Red Hills Information Center to Hohokam Road. Turn right. The Hugh Norris Trailhead is 0.8 of a mile ahead. There is a small parking area on the right.

Fees: Entrance to Saguaro National Park is $10 for any privately owned vehicle or motorcycle and $5 for any individual on foot or bicycle. Entry is valid for seven days. Several passes are also available: Saguaro National Park Annual Pass, $25, is valid for one year from the date of purchase; America the Beautiful Annual Pass, $80; America the Beautiful, Senior Pass, $10, is a lifetime pass to National Park and Recreation Areas for US citizens age 62 and over; and the Access Pass, a lifetime pass for US citizens or permanent residents with permanent disabilities. Passes may be purchased at the Saguaro National Park Visitor Centers.

■ ■ ■

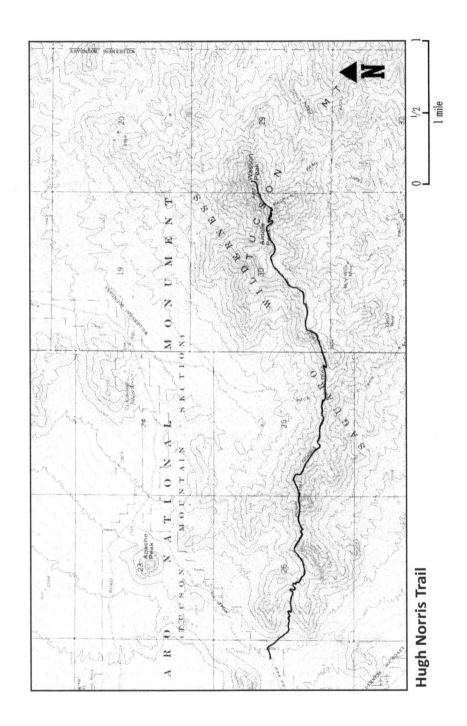

Hugh Norris Trail

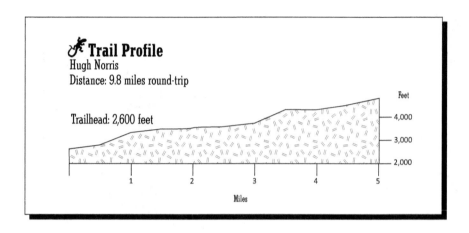

My favorite route to the summit of Wasson Peak is the Hugh Norris Trail. Although longer than other routes, the climb is gradual, and the views from the ridges are spectacular. Wasson Peak offers an unforgettable 360-degree view of the Tucson valley.

This excellent trail is named for Hugh Norris, a Tohono O'odham police chief. The peak it reaches was named for John Wasson, a colorful, often controversial, early editor of the *Tucson Citizen*, who, much to his surprise, was appointed surveyor general of the Arizona Territory in 1870. Although he had absolutely no experience in the field, he retained the position until 1882, when he moved to California.

Signs at the beginning of the Hugh Norris Trail are typical of the trailheads in the Saguaro National Park. Pets are prohibited, as are bicycles, motor vehicles, and weapons. A map depicts the trails of the Park, listing the distances in both miles and kilometers. There is also a trail register. It's fun to read the register and note where the hikers came from, especially in winter, when people converge on Tucson from all over the United States and world. These registers serve other purposes. The rangers can judge trail usage, and, in case of the necessity for a search and rescue operation, searchers can tell if the lost hiker did indeed go on this trail. A final sign indicates that the trailhead elevation is 2,600 feet.

The trail climbs gradually at first and then becomes steeper. The only difficulty is stepping over the rocks placed across the trail to pre-

Tucson and the Santa Catalinas from Wasson Peak.

vent erosion. After about a quarter of a mile the trail crosses a deep, sandy drainage, climbs out, and heads up the canyon directly between two ridges. As you gain in elevation, look back at the saguaro forest. There is no place like this in the world. Thousands of giant saguaros spread across the bajada, a Spanish term indicating the transition zone between the mountain and the valley. Beyond the saguaros are the farms of Avra Valley. What appears to be a very straight road across the edge of the farm area is actually the canal of the Central Arizona Project (CAP), which delivers water from the Colorado River to Phoenix and Tucson. In Tucson, CAP water is blended with ground water before being delivered to homes.

As the drainage narrows, the trail steepens and becomes a series of switchbacks that lead to the top of the ridge. To the north, where the walls of the drainage provide protection for the tiny saguaro seeds, there are many young saguaros. This is a pretty, quiet area. The sounds of planes overhead and the occasional pecking of a woodpecker or chirping of other birds is all you hear. You can easily reach the top of this first ridge in forty-five minutes.

On top of the ridge, the trail turns to the right and is level, then quickly turns left, around the side, and gradually switchbacks to the top of a small saddle. In this saddle there are several side paths that lead to the viewpoints on both sides of the saddle, where there are many boulders that make a good lunch or snack spot.

From this saddle the trail descends briefly, crosses a longer saddle, and begins a long trek along the north side of the ridge. This is a very pleasant portion of the trail. There is some slight elevation gain but nothing serious. The trail is now basically a ridge trail, meandering from one side of the ridge to the other and occasionally going along the top. The views change from one side to the other, first the Catalinas, then Picacho Peak, then the Santa Ritas or Rincons. Below and to the northwest, the Sendero Esperanza Trail winds its way through the basin and up the ridge. Far to the north and high on the ridge, you can see where the Hugh Norris Trail continues its climb to Wasson Peak.

After leveling out on top of the ridge, the trail passes a fenced mine to the right with the warning sign that says, "Peligro Excavacion" or "Danger Excavation." Yet there are signs of where people have crawled under the fence to explore just a little farther, a dangerous practice that has led to the loss of several lives in the Tucson Mountains. A quarter of a mile past the pit and around the east side of the ridge is a signed trail intersection.

This is a good resting spot and meeting place for people who have arranged car swaps to prevent the retracing of steps. For example, one car can be left at the Sendero Esperanza Trailhead, another at Hugh Norris, and still another at King Canyon. All hikers can converge on Wasson Peak and return by a different route. The Hugh Norris Trail continues straight past the intersection and along the ridge for 2.2 miles to the summit of Wasson Peak.

From the intersection, it is a gradual climb along the northwestern side of the ridge. As on the first section of the trail, the rocks placed on the trail for erosion control are the only problem with the trail. After half a mile the trail crosses a short saddle, from which the hiker can see both sides of the mountain. As you look ahead to the peaks, it is difficult to figure out which one is actually Wasson. It is not the one it appears to be, but the peak farthest away and to the left. After the saddle the trail crosses back to the western side of the ridge. At a small sign marking the 4,000-foot elevation level, the trail turns to the right and quickly left across another short saddle, following the east side of the ridge along a smooth, sandy trail.

The trail from this point again meanders from one side of the ridge to the other, interspersed with small saddles. It is smooth and not at all difficult. From this portion of the trail you can see more extensive evidence of the mining that took place in the Tucson Mountains in the early 1900s and again in the 1940s.

Most of the last half mile of the trail is a series of steep switchbacks. The large rock outcropping directly ahead of the switchbacks is not Wasson Peak, as you will shortly realize, although from the switchbacks it appears to be the high point. Wasson Peak is now visible on the left. At the top of the switchbacks is a signed trail intersection. The King Canyon trailhead is 3.2 miles down the other side of the ridge. The Hugh Norris Trail continues an easy 0.3 of a mile to the summit.

Right before the summit is a trail sign-in box. It is interesting to read the comments of hikers who have reached this vantage point. People from all over the United States have signed the trail registers, with comments like "Better than Mount Rainier!" "A fantastic day," and frequently, just "Wow!" On a clear day, you can see all of Tucson and the surrounding mountains. The comments are understandable.

King Canyon Trail

General Description: A hike up a canyon past petroglyphs and old mines, to the intersection of the Hugh Norris Trail, near the top of Wasson Peak

Difficulty: Moderate, short areas of moderate climbing

Best Time of Year to Hike: Winter

Length: 7 miles round-trip

Miles to Trailhead from Speedway/Campbell Intersection: 14.6 miles

Directions to Trailhead from Speedway/Campbell Intersection: Go west on Speedway, over Gates Pass to the intersection of Kinney Road. Turn right on Kinney Road, to the Arizona-Sonora Desert Museum. The parking area for the King Canyon Trail is 0.1 of a mile past the entrance to the museum and on the right.

Fees: Entrance to Saguaro National Park is $10 for any privately owned vehicle or motorcycle and $5 for any individual on foot or bicycle. Entry is valid for seven days. Several passes are also available: Saguaro National Park Annual Pass, $25, is valid for one year from the date of purchase; America the Beautiful Annual Pass, $80; America the Beautiful, Senior Pass, $10, is a lifetime pass to National Park and Recreation Areas for US citizens age 62 and over; and the Access Pass, a lifetime pass for US citizens or permanent residents with permanent disabilities. Passes may be purchased at the Saguaro National Park Visitor Centers.

■　■　■

In 1917 the Copper King Mine was developed in this canyon. Although the mine has been long since abandoned, the trail up the canyon now bears the name of the mine and is known as the King Canyon Trail. In

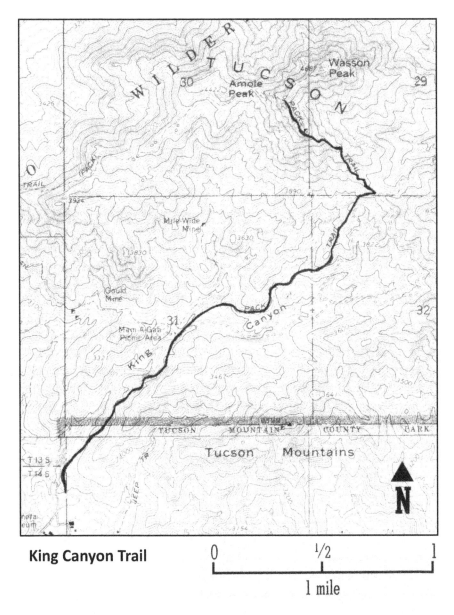

King Canyon Trail   0   ¹/₂   1

1 mile

combination with the Hugh Norris Trail, the King Canyon Trail is the shortest route to the summit of Wasson Peak.

Signs at the trailhead warn about the open mine shafts. A sign also notes that one quart of water is the minimum that a hiker should carry to hike this trail. On warm days, one quart is not enough. It is always

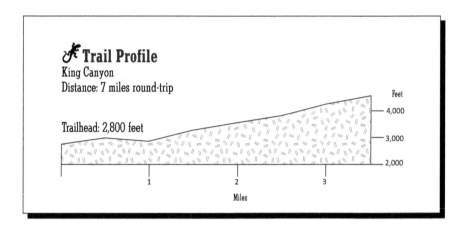

ॐ **Trail Profile**
King Canyon
Distance: 7 miles round-trip

better to have more water than necessary. The sign also indicates that King Canyon has the only permanent source of water in the Tucson Mountains, but don't count on finding it.

The trail begins as an old jeep road and for the first mile is a wide, rocky walk along the west side of the ridge. Most of the year the canyon drainage is dry, but in times of heavy rain, the rush of water would be an awesome sight. Soon you can see the picnic shelter of the Mam-A-Gah picnic area and the rock building that serves as a rest room below it.

As the road approaches the intersection, it drops into and crosses the canyon. Off the trail and to the left, about quarter of a mile down the canyon drainage and immediately past a small dam, are many petroglyphs. On both sides of the drainage are many etched drawings that were made by Hohokam Indians, who lived in these mountains from 300 A.D. to 1500 A.D. Some of the drawings are intricate, and others look like random scribbling. If you are hiking just the King Canyon Trail, you can save this exploration for the return trip, because the wash can be followed almost to the highway, where a path leads up to the parking lot. If you are trading keys with a fellow hiker and will not return by this route, it is worth the short side trip to see the petroglyphs.

As you cross the canyon bottom, a short side trail to the left leads up to the Mam-A-Gah picnic area, where there are six tables and one ramada (shelter). This frequently used picnic area is named for the "deer dance" of the Tohono O'odham Indians. The King Canyon Trail turns to the right, past the rest rooms.

Petroglyphs near the King Canyon Trail.

The Sendero Esperanza Trailhead is immediately past the rest rooms and to the left. King Canyon Trail is straight ahead and, as the sign indicates, reaches Wasson Peak in 2.6 miles.

Past the intersection, the trail narrows and continues up the canyon. No longer a jeep road, the trail is now very rocky, and sturdy hiking boots are a necessity. In about 200 yards the trail crosses another drainage and then goes along a low ridge between King Canyon and the side drainage for a short distance, before beginning to climb. To the east is an old mine road built when hope was high for the mining potential in these mountains.

The Mile Wide Mining Company owned the claims in this area, and geologist reports were optimistic. Charles F. Willis, geologist and editor of the *Arizona Mining Journal*, said in August 1916, "the Mile Wide Copper Company is destined to become one of the large producers for which the State of Arizona is so well known . . . the property has everything pointing toward success and absolutely none of the signboards of failure." The company named their main mine the Copper King, lowered shafts to a depth of 400 feet, and excavated tunnels. Mining was carried out in 1917 and 1918 and again briefly in 1943, but was never the hoped-for success. The Copper King passed through several owners before being abandoned altogether, achieving a total production of only 1,400 tons. All that remains today are the scars.

The trail continues to climb along the east side of the hill and is easy to follow. In about a mile, it reaches the top of the ridge and again becomes an abandoned road. If you are hiking here in early spring, which arrives in late February, this area is usually dotted with wildflowers. If the rains have been sufficient and the winter not too cold, tiny golden poppies peak up through the rocks. Look closely and you will see other varieties. It is one of the mysteries of nature that these flowers can survive the harsh conditions that exist in these mountains.

The road winds around the side of the hill and comes to the intersection of the Sweetwater Trail. Now, for the first time on the King Canyon Trail, you can see the other side of the mountain and the western end of the Santa Catalina Range. It is now only 1.2 miles to Wasson Peak; however, it is a steep 1.2 miles.

From this intersection the trail climbs steeply to the west. The main obstacles on the trail are the large rocks carefully placed to prevent erosion. The peak directly above you is not Wasson. As you climb, the trail becomes a series of switchbacks that climb steadily. There are several fenced mine shafts along this portion of the trail, all with warning signs. As you switchback up the trail, more mines become visible, some in places that look totally inaccessible. You wonder why that particular site was chosen, since the terrain is so rugged and barren.

As the trail reaches the top of the switchbacks, most of the city is visible and Wasson Peak stands out to the north. As the trail levels along the north side of the ridge, you can see the trail intersection sign ahead. Another fenced mine is on the right, with the warning sign in Spanish, "Peligro Excavacion." Past this mine, the trail is level briefly and then climbs in a few switchbacks to the trail intersection. This is the end of the King Canyon Trail. To reach Wasson Peak, follow the Hugh Norris Trail 0.3 of a mile to the summit. The final section is easy and well worth the brief climb required.

Ez-Kim-In-Zin Picnic Area to Signal Hill

General Description: A hike through a desert wash to the summit of Signal Hill, where prehistoric people etched hundreds of pictographs

Difficulty: Easy; over half of the hike is in a sandy wash

Best Time of Year to Hike: Late fall, winter, early spring

Length: 3.8 miles one-way, car exchange

Miles to Trailhead from Speedway/Campbell Intersection: 24 miles

Directions to Trailhead from Speedway/Campbell Intersection: Go west on Speedway to Gates Pass. Speedway becomes Gates Pass Road. Continue on Gates Pass Road to Kinney Road. Turn right. Follow Kinney Road past the Arizona-Sonora Desert Museum and the Red Hills Information Center until the intersection of Kinney and Sandario Road. Turn right on Sandario Road. Leave one vehicle at the Signal Hill Picnic Area. Continue on Golden Gate Road to the Ez-Kim-In-Zin Picnic Area. The trail begins at the trailhead sign on the left just as you enter the picnic area. Park in the parking area and walk back to the trailhead sign to begin the hike.

Fees: Entrance to Saguaro National Park is $10 for any privately owned vehicle or motorcycle and $5 for any individual on foot or bicycle. Entry is valid for seven days. Several passes are also available: Saguaro National Park Annual Pass, $25, is valid for one year from the date of purchase; America the Beautiful Annual Pass, $80; America the Beautiful, Senior Pass, $10, is a lifetime pass to National Park and Recreation Areas for US citizens age 62 and over; and the Access Pass, a lifetime pass for US citizens or permanent residents with permanent disabilities. Passes may be purchased at the Saguaro National Park Visitor Centers.

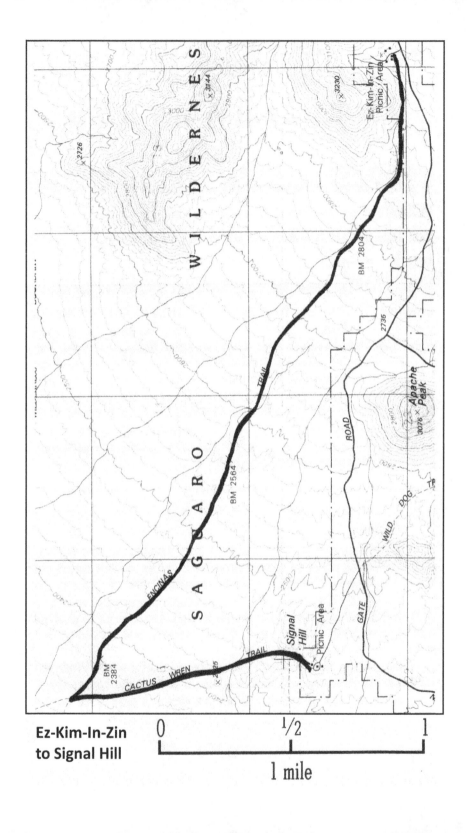

**Ez-Kim-In-Zin
to Signal Hill**

0   1/2   1

1 mile

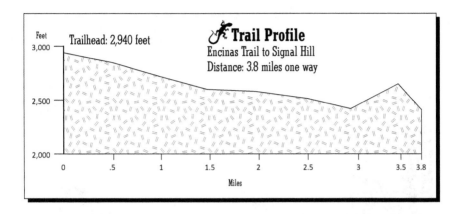

Feet
3,000

Trailhead: 2,940 feet

🦎 **Trail Profile**
Encinas Trail to Signal Hill
Distance: 3.8 miles one way

2,500

2,000

0   .5   1   1.5   2   2.5   3   3.5 3.8

Miles

■ ■ ■

Civilian Conservation Corps (CCC) members built the Ez-Kim-In-Zin Picnic Area, named for a leader of the Aravaipa Apache Nation, in the 1930s as part of a federal program to provide work during the Great Depression. Only physically fit males between the ages of 18 and 25 were eligible for the program. Participants agreed to send $25 of their $30 monthly paycheck home to their families. CCC workers used natural stone to build picnic tables, shelters, and restrooms that have stood the test of time.

The Encinas Trail primarily follows the route of a wash. While the trail may not have the spectacular views of trails in the higher elevations of the Tucson Mountains, it offers a close-up look at life on the desert floor. It's name is Spanish for evergreen or oak.

Imagine this scene a thousand years ago when shallow water flowed constantly in this wash and a prehistoric people we call Hohokam built their homes nearby. Today the wash is dry except when water flows briefly after a fierce summer storm.

The best time to hike the Encinas Trail is on a warm early spring day when desert wildflowers are beginning to bloom. Since much of the trail is sandy and slows your pace, it helps to walk on the edges of the wash where the soil is firmer. The trail is well-marked. When the wash curves, a sign in the middle of the wash indicates the direction of the trail.

Saguaro in every stage of development grow near the wash. There are giants that are as old as 200 years. Small saguaro thrive under *nurse*

Hiker studying "ghost" saguaro on the Encinas Trail.

trees; palo verde and mesquite trees are called *nurse* trees because they provide protection for the small saguaro. Saguaro in various stages of dying are scattered about, some with rotting flesh and others with only the ribs remaining. A "ghost" saguaro with its ribs flared out like an upside down umbrella stands on the left of the wash. When breezes blow the ribs make a sound like bones rattling. A hiker, passing this way at dusk, may imagine a ghost is nearby.

On my first hike on the Encinas Trail, about halfway down the wash, I saw a kit fox. This was the first time I had ever seen a kit fox in the wild. The usually nocturnal fox stands only one foot tall and weighs from four to five pounds. Kit foxes prey on jackrabbits, ground squirrels, mice, kangaroo rats, lizards, and insects. They do not need freestanding water. They are able to survive on what moisture they get from their prey.

As the wash narrows, the saguaro thin out and the vegetation becomes primarily cholla of assorted varieties. Large fishhook barrel cacti lean to the south into the sun. To the north the stark outline of Picacho Peak is prominent on the horizon. The farms of Avra Valley and the Silverbell Mine are visible to the west.

After 1.9 miles, a sign in the middle of the wash indicates that the Signal Hill Picnic Area is to the left 0.9 miles on the Cactus Wren Trail. Turn here. Thankfully out of the sand, the now rocky trail begins a gradual climb to Signal Hill. As we climb, the views expand to the north and west.

A lucky hiker may see a cactus wren, the state bird of Arizona. Mary Taylor Gray, in her *Watchable Birds of the Southwest*, describes the cactus wren as "a large wren with a rusty brown back streaked with white, dark cap with conspicuous white eyebrow, dark brown wings and tail with white bars, and paler undersides with heavy speckled breast." Their nests are large—as much as a foot in diameter—and generally built in cholla cactus, yucca, catclaw, or other desert plants. Cactus wrens raise as many as three families a year. While the female is incubating the first clutch of eggs, the male begins building a second nest for the next brood.

The trail climbs steeply to the top of a hill. This hill is known as Signal Hill because of the petroglyphs etched in the rocks by prehistoric peoples, probably the Hohokam who lived in the area from approximately 300 A.D. to 1500 A.D. No one knows the meaning of the designs, but it is believed that some of the drawings could be signals or messages to people passing by the area.

Hohokam means "the people who have gone." Although it is possible that the present day Indian tribe living near Tucson, the Tohono O'odham, are descendants of the Hohokam, no one knows for certain. If the Hohokam did, in fact, disappear, the cause of their disappearance is also unknown.

Hopefully, you have left a vehicle at the Signal Hill Picnic Area and will drive back to Ez-Kim-In-Zin Picnic Area. Otherwise, turn around and head back down Signal Hill and up the Encinas Trail. That's much more pleasant than walking back on Golden Gate Road.

Sendero Esperanza Trail

General Description: A short trail across a ridge, with great views in all directions

Difficulty: Moderate, some areas of steep switchbacks

Best Time of Year to Hike: Winter

Length: 3.2 miles one way

Miles to Trailhead from Speedway/Campbell Intersection: 22.2 miles

Directions to Trailhead from Speedway/Campbell Intersection: Go west on Speedway, over Gates Pass, until you reach the intersection of Kinney Road. Just past the Arizona-Sonora Desert Museum, look for the turn into Saguaro National Park. Drive past the Red Hills Information Center. Turn right on Hohokam Road. Hohokam Road is unpaved and becomes one way after the Hugh Norris Trailhead. Turn right on Golden Gate Road, to the parking area for the Sendero Esperanza Trailhead. (The ideal way to do this hike is to leave a vehicle at the King Canyon Trailhead, 0.1 of a mile on the right, past the Arizona-Sonora Desert Museum, and drive back to pick up the first car or arrange a key swap with friends.)

Fees: Entrance to Saguaro National Park is $10 for any privately owned vehicle or motorcycle and $5 for any individual on foot or bicycle. Entry is valid for seven days. Several passes are also available: Saguaro National Park Annual Pass, $25, is valid for one year from the date of purchase; America the Beautiful Annual Pass, $80; America the Beautiful, Senior Pass, $10, is a lifetime pass to National Park and Recreation Areas for US citizens age 62 and over; and the Access Pass, a lifetime pass for US citizens or permanent residents with permanent disabilities. Passes may be purchased at the Saguaro National Park Visitor Centers.

Esperanza is Spanish for "hope," thus, *Sendero Esperanza* is the trail of hope. How this name came to be attached to this particular trail is unclear, but one can speculate that, because the trail leads to a large mine, someone once hoped to find riches at the end of the trail!

The Sendero Esperanza Trail climbs the ridge directly to the east of the trailhead and descends on the other side, past the extensive workings of the old Gould Mine, ending at the intersection of the King Canyon Trail, 1 mile north of the Arizona-Sonora Desert Museum. After 1.8 miles, the Sendero Esperanza Trail intersects with the Hugh Norris Trail and makes an excellent route to the top of Wasson Peak. From the parking area to Wasson Peak (via the Sendero Esperanza and Hugh Norris Trails), the distance is 4 miles.

Signs at the parking area give a detailed map of the trail system. Pay careful attention to the "Open Mine Shafts—Please Stay on Trail" warning. There are many abandoned mine shafts in the area and lives have been lost by curious explorers who just couldn't resist one more step.

The Sendero Esperanza Trail is flat and sandy for almost the first mile, as it follows a drainage and gains elevation gradually. After the first mile the trail narrows and turns gradually to the right for a short distance, before beginning to climb the switchbacks to the left.

As you look toward the mountain, you can see the ridge that you are about to climb. As you begin to climb the switchbacks, the trail becomes quite rocky in places. The views to the north and northwest are great on a clear day. Depending on the time of year, the fields near Marana are squares of green or brown. The triangular outline of Picacho Peak stands out forty miles north of Tucson. Now a state park, the peak stands in history, a bit erroneously, as the westernmost battle of the Civil War.

As you top the ridge, you come to the well-marked intersection of the Hugh Norris and Sendero Esperanza Trails. From this vantage point, you can see The Red Hills Information Center, the traffic on Kinney Road, and the Santa Rita Mountains, to the south. Mount Wrightson and Mount Hopkins are the dominant peaks in this range. The Sendero Esperanza Trail drops to the other side of the ridge, past the Mam-A-Gah Picnic Area, to intersect with the King Canyon Trail.

The trail descends immediately down the west side of the ridge. The trail is quite rocky and can be treacherous, because it switchbacks

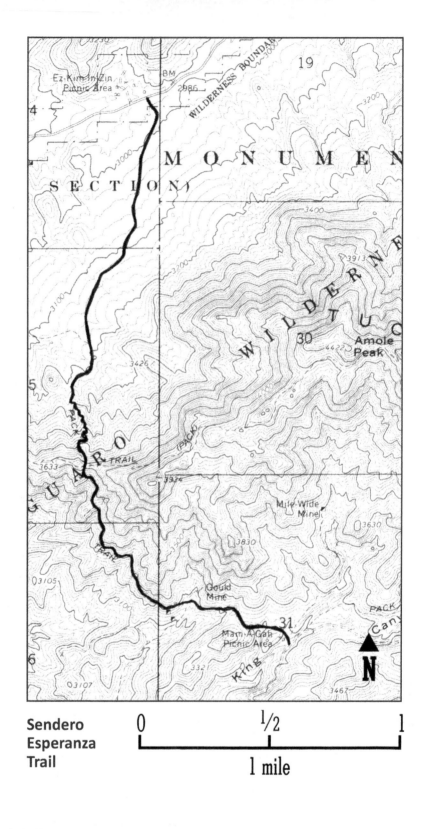

Sendero
Esperanza
Trail

0   ¹/₂   1

1 mile

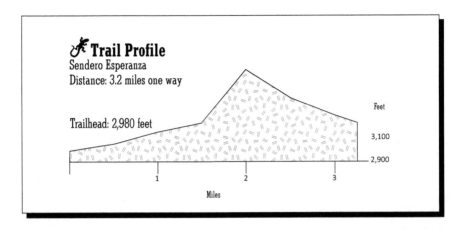

⚡ Trail Profile
Sendero Esperanza
Distance: 3.2 miles one way

Trailhead: 2,980 feet

and curves downward quickly. This rocky portion is short and after a quarter of a mile, the trail intersects with an old mine road. The Sendero Esperanza Trail goes to the left. The old road is smooth and easy to walk on. It remains level, or a very gradual downhill, for a quarter of a mile or so. There are abandoned mines along the trail. These mines were operated in the days before environmental protection was an issue, so there are many scars.

The views from the road are excellent. Kitt and Baboquivari Peaks stand out in the distance. The hills, made red by iron oxide, to the west are distinct. There are many old weather-beaten saguaros along the road.

Near the bottom of the hill is what remains of the Gould Mine. The *Arizona Daily Star* carried enthusiastic reports of the potential of the mine, stating on May 17, 1905, "the Gould people talk as if they have the biggest bonanza in the territory." By December 21, reports said, "the Gould was working day and night." On July 7, 1907, the *Star* reported "15 wagons carrying ore from the Gould Mine to the Southern Pacific for shipment to El Paso." The Gould Mine worked at a depth of 360 feet and was in production intermittently from 1905 until 1912. Despite the optimism, the total production of the Gould Mine was only 1,500 tons. The owners were forced into bankruptcy in 1915. A fenced shaft, partially covered by boards, a few old beams on the side of the hill, and, 100 yards past the mine, a stone powder house, are all that remain of the Gould Mine today.

Powder House—Gould Mine, Sendero Esperanza Trail.

Just past the Gould Mine, the road crosses a deep drainage that runs immediately after a rain. On both sides of the drainage is evidence of other mines. Across the drainage the trail climbs gradually. As you round the bend, the shelter and picnic tables of the Mam-A-Gah picnic area are visible. This is a popular destination for hikers entering from the King Canyon trailhead. As the trail crosses a small drainage, you will notice an unmarked path to the right that leads to the picnic area. The trail continues straight ahead, and in about 200 yards you will come to the official signed path that leads up to the picnic tables. The Sendero Esperanza Trail ends 200 yards past this sign.

A sign indicates that the Arizona-Sonora Desert Museum is a mile ahead. The King Canyon trailhead is 0.9 of a mile along the road across the wash. If you are doing a key swap or have a vehicle at the King Canyon trailhead, continue on the King Canyon Trail to the parking area; otherwise return to the Sendero Esperanza Trailhead by retracing your steps.

Sweetwater Trail

General Description: An enjoyable climb through one of the most varied stands of saguaro in the Tucson Mountains

Difficulty: Difficult

Best Time of Year to Hike: Spring, fall, winter

Length: 6.4 miles round-trip

Miles to Trailhead from Speedway/Campbell Intersection: 15 miles

Directions to Trailhead from Speedway/Campbell Intersection: Drive north on Campbell Avenue to Fort Lowell Road. Turn left on Fort Lowell Road to Stone Avenue. Turn right on Stone Avenue to Wetmore Road. Turn left on Wetmore Road. Continue on Wetmore to Romero Road. Turn right on Romero. Romero becomes Ruthrauff at the curve, which becomes El Camino del Cerro after passing under Interstate 10. Continue on El Camino del Cerro until it dead-ends at the trailhead. A paved trailhead parking area has room for fifteen cars and two horsetrailers.

Fees: Entrance to Saguaro National Park is $10 for any privately owned vehicle or motorcycle and $5 for any individual on foot or bicycle. Entry is valid for seven days. Several passes are also available: Saguaro National Park Annual Pass, $25, is valid for one year from the date of purchase; America the Beautiful Annual Pass, $80; America the Beautiful, Senior Pass, $10, is a lifetime pass to National Park and Recreation Areas for US citizens age 62 and over; and the Access Pass, a lifetime pass for US citizens or permanent residents with permanent disabilities. Passes may be purchased at the Saguaro National Park Visitor Centers.

■ ■ ■

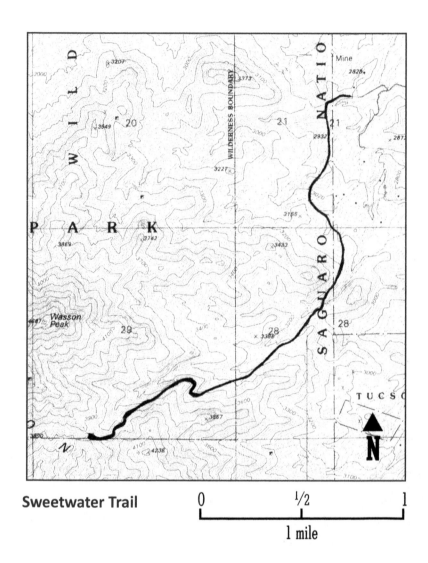

Sweetwater Trail

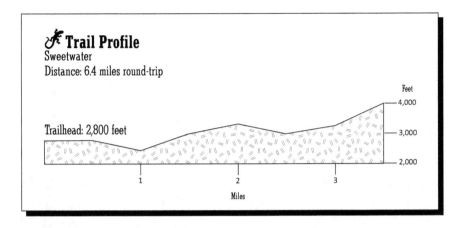

𖤐 **Trail Profile**
Sweetwater
Distance: 6.4 miles round-trip

Find a guide to plants of the Sonoran Desert and head for the Sweetwater Trail. It's a virtual botanical classroom, with emphasis on saguaro in various stages of growth.

This trail was for a long time inaccessible because it required crossing private land to reach the trailhead. A new trailhead parking area and connecting link, constructed as a joint effort between Pima County and the Saguaro National Park, now makes the Sweetwater Trail accessible to hikers and horseback riders. A sign at the trailhead indicates that the Sweetwater Trail meets the King Canyon Trail in 3.4 miles. From this intersection, it is only 1.2 miles to Wasson Peak, the high point of the Tucson Mountains.

The trail begins as a level walk along a low ridge. In about 0.2 mile a sign indicates that the Sweetwater Trail turns left and drops into a deep wash. After crossing the wash, the trail climbs the ridge and provides excellent views of the city to the east and Wasson Peak to the west. It is easy to follow and in one section includes a series of switchbacks and steps. Side trails have been disguised by extensive plantings of prickly pear and cholla.

A little over halfway into the hike, the new section of the trail joins the original trail and becomes more difficult to hike. The older trail is narrow and rocky in comparison with the wider and smoother new section. Still, it is relatively easy and, as the trail climbs toward the saddle, provides ever more dramatic views of the Tucson Valley to the east and Wasson Peak to the northwest.

On the hike to Wasson Peak via Sweetwater.

Enjoying being on the summit of Wasson Peak.

Of particular interest is the large number of saguaro in all stages of growth. The saguaro thrives on southern exposures and near the washes. Younger plants from one to three feet tall are abundant, as are several giants, which must be more than one hundred years old. Look for a large crested saguaro where the trail drops into a large wash.

The Sweetwater Trail ends in a small saddle. From here it is possible to continue on to Wasson Peak via the King Canyon and Hugh Norris Trails, or to go down the mountain on the King Canyon Trail to the parking area across the road from the Arizona-Sonora Desert Museum. The trail network in the Saguaro National Park provides numerous possibilities for key exchanges. Wasson Peak can be reached from the King Canyon, Hugh Norris, Sendero Esperanza, and Sweetwater trailheads.

Roadrunner–Panther Peak Wash–Cam-Boh Trail Loop

General Description: A loop hike in a scenic area that includes dramatic views of Panther Peak

Difficulty: Easy; part of the loop is in a sandy wash

Best Time of Year to Hike: Late fall, winter, early spring

Length: 4.6-mile loop

Miles to Trailhead from Speedway/Campbell Intersection: 22.5 miles

Directions to Trailhead from Speedway/Campbell Intersection: Go north on Campbell Avenue to Skyline Drive. Turn left. Skyline Drive becomes Ina Road. Continue on Ina Road, passing under Interstate 10 until the intersection of Ina and Wade roads. Turn left on Wade Road. Follow Wade Road for 0.1 mile, then turn right on Picture Rocks Road. Continue on Picture Rocks Road to the Cam-Boh Picnic Area, which is on the left. Park your vehicle near the restrooms. Note: Cam-Boh Picnic Area is in Saguaro National Park. If you pass signs indicating the park boundary, you have passed the picnic area.

Fees: Entrance to Saguaro National Park is $10 for any privately owned vehicle or motorcycle and $5 for any individual on foot or bicycle. Entry is valid for seven days. Several passes are also available: Saguaro National Park Annual Pass, $25, is valid for one year from the date of purchase; America the Beautiful Annual Pass, $80; America the Beautiful, Senior Pass, $10, is a lifetime pass to National Park and Recreation Areas for US citizens age 62 and over; and the Access Pass, a lifetime pass for US citizens or permanent residents with permanent disabilities. Passes may be purchased at the Saguaro National Park Visitor Centers.

■   ■   ■

Seventy million years ago the rugged mountains in this area were located twenty miles to the northeast on top of the Santa Catalina Mountains. A volcano, perhaps 1,000 times more powerful than Mount St. Helens, erupted where the Catalinas stand today. Over the next 40 million years, the huge granite mass of the Catalinas rose until the entire volcanic complex slid off the mountains to form what we now call the Tucson Mountains. A hike along the Roadrunner–Panther Peak Wash–Cam-Boh Loop provides excellent views of the results of this activity.

Roadrunner Trail begins directly across the road from the Cam-Boh Picnic Area. Cross carefully, as Picture Rocks Road is heavily traveled, often at speeds that exceed the limit. The trail heads directly toward Panther Peak and follows the boundary of Saguaro National Park West. While some of the trail is in a sandy wash, most of the trail is rocky. As you will note, the trail is popular with horseback riders.

True to the trail's name, roadrunners thrive in this area. Unlike the beeping roadrunner in the roadrunner cartoon, the real roadrunner makes a series of cooing sounds like a dove. If you're lucky, you'll catch a glimpse of a roadrunner, a brownish-gray bird about the size of a scrawny chicken. The roadrunner prefers walking or running to flying and can attain speeds as high as seventeen miles per hour. Remember, Wile E. Coyote never caught the roadrunner! A roadrunner's favorite meal is a rattlesnake, which he grabs by the tail and kills by cracking the snake like a whip. When he can't find a rattlesnake for dinner, a lizard will do, as will various insects.

As you hike along this section, look north toward the stark triangular outline of Picacho Peak, known for its splendid display of Mexican poppies in the spring. Closer in are what remains of Twin Peaks, one of which has been nearly leveled in a limestone mining operation. As you get closer to the mountains and Panther Peak Wash, the vegetation changes. The saguaro thin out and are replaced by a forest of chain fruit cholla. Across the wash and near the cliffs the saguaros thrive once again.

When you reach Panther Peak Wash, a sign indicates that it is 1.9 miles to the Cam-Boh (Tohono O'odham for "camp") Trail. Take a minute and imagine Panther Peak fifty years ago when panthers stood on the peak looking for their prey. Panthers weigh an average of 125 pounds and frequent rugged mountain areas.

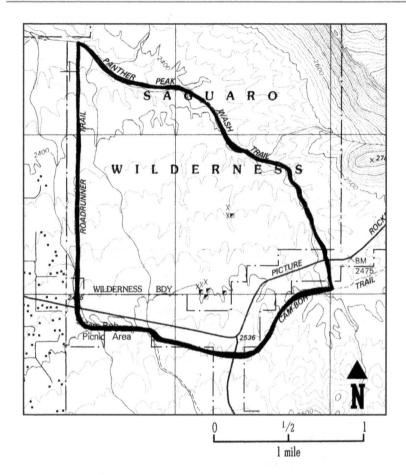

0   ¹/₂   1

1 mile

Roadrunner–Panther Peak Wash–Cam-Boh Loop

Known by other names—most commonly the mountain lion, but also cougar and puma—panthers were once plentiful across the entire United States. However, their propensity for killing cattle and the farmer's response soon eliminated panthers in the eastern United States. The few remaining panthers live in mountainous regions of the West.

In many western states, particularly Arizona, the federal government's Animal Damage Control program (now called Wildlife Services)

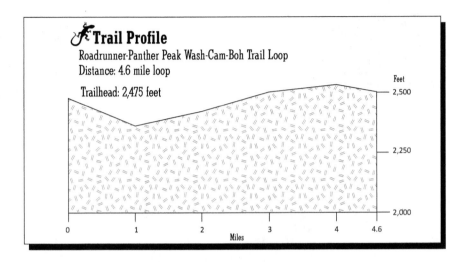

Trail Profile
Roadrunner-Panther Peak Wash-Cam-Boh Trail Loop
Distance: 4.6 mile loop

Trailhead: 2,475 feet

paid bounties to kill panthers. On the North Rim of the Grand Canyon, Game Warden Jim Owens killed more than 1,200 panthers from 1909 to 1917. In southeastern Arizona, bounty hunters shot and killed 50 panthers between 1988 and 1990. Protests by environmental groups led to the elimination of the bounty program.

Still, survival of panthers in the Tucson Mountains is in doubt. A February 15, 2003, article in the *Arizona Daily Star* by Mitch Tobin, "Mountain Lions Squeezed," reported that panthers are rapidly losing habitat in the Tucson Mountains. A 2010 study by the University of Arizona School of Natural Resources and Environment Wild Cat Research and Conservation photographed only four panthers remaining in the Tucson Mountains.

Turn right and follow Panther Peak Wash Trail. The trail follows the route of the wash and walking in sand slows your pace. Walk quietly and you may see a group of javelinas. Washes are javelina highways!

When you hear traffic from Picture Rocks Road, look on the left for the trail to leave the wash. When I last hiked this trail, this turnoff was marked by large cairns made of broken rocks and bricks. Cross Picture Rocks Road and join the Cam-Boh Trail back to the picnic area. At the trail sign, turn right.

Hiker looking at Panther Peak on the Roadrunner–
Panther Peak Wash–Cam-Boh Trail Loop.

As on other trails in the lower elevations of the Tucson Mountains, it is the little things that make this hike worthwhile. An example is the funnel web spider's web. Made of silk, the web looks like a flat funnel about six inches in diameter with the spout inserted in the spider's nest. An unsuspecting insect investigating the funnel soon finds himself trapped.

Before reaching the picnic area, the Cam-Boh Trail crosses Golden Gate Road and Prophecy Wash. It also passes an old mine that is fenced with signs indicating "Danger Open Shaft." As the trail nears the picnic area, steps are carved into the trail. Hike finished, find your vehicle and head into the crossroads town of Picture Rocks for a post-hike snack.

David Yetman Trail

General Description: An easy walk through typical vegetation of the Sonoran Desert

Difficulty: Moderate, few areas with slight elevation gain

Best Time of Year to Hike: Winter, early spring, late fall

Length: 5.4 miles, with two vehicles

Miles to Trailhead from Speedway/Campbell Intersection: 10.1 miles to parking area on west side of Gates Pass

Directions to Trailhead from Speedway/Campbell Intersection: The Yetman Trail has two trailheads. It is possible to leave cars at each trailhead and work out combinations that enable you not to have to retrace steps. A good combination that makes most of the hike downhill is to leave a vehicle at the Camino de Oeste Trailhead and continue to the Gates Pass Trailhead. To do this from the Speedway/Campbell intersection, go west on Speedway. Shortly after passing the West Anklam Road/Speedway intersection, turn left on Camino de Oeste. Drive carefully up the unpaved road, until it dead-ends with a parking area on the right and leave a vehicle. Continue on Speedway, which is now called Gates Pass Road, across Gates Pass and down the west side of the mountain, to a large parking area on the left, almost at the bottom of the mountain. This is the starting point for the David Yetman Trail.

■　■　■

David Yetman was a member of the Pima County Board of Supervisors from 1977 to 1988. Sometimes controversial, Yetman became known for his fervent defense of the environment. The Yetman Trail,

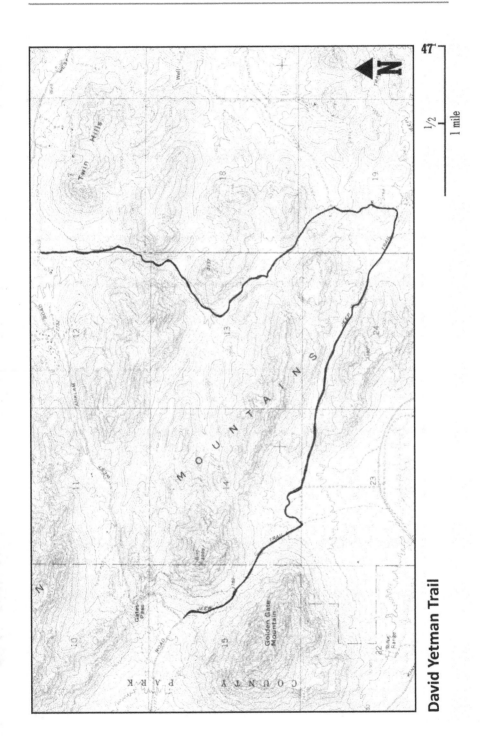

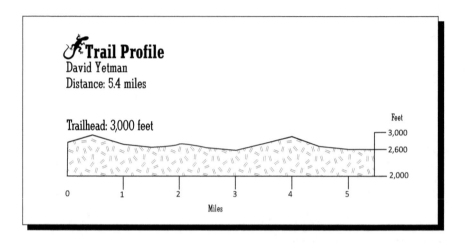

Trail Profile
David Yetman
Distance: 5.4 miles

Trailhead: 3,000 feet

Feet
— 3,000
— 2,600
— 2,000

0   1   2   3   4   5

Miles

which crosses a lovely area in the Tucson Mountains, was named in his honor when he retired from the Board of Supervisors.

The David Yetman Trail is marked by a sign on the left. The trail begins on an old mine, or jeep, road. After about three-quarters of a mile, signs indicate the intersection of three trails—the Golden Gate Trail to the right, the Gates Pass Trail to the left, and the David Yetman Trail straight ahead.

The Yetman Trail goes through the pass and continues downhill. This is an easy trail and is perfect for people who want to become better acquainted with the Sonoran Desert without too much elevation gain. This portion goes through a stand of teddy bear cholla. In about 0.5 of a mile a sign indicates that the Yetman Trail bears to the left. This portion of the trail is well marked as it meanders in and out of small drainages. The trail is a favorite of mountain bikers, and often side trails have been created to climb small hills. Watch carefully for the correct route.

After approximately 0.8 of a mile the Yetman Trail bears to the left. Here the trail crosses several washes before climbing briefly, albeit steeply, to the side of a ridge. Notice that the side of the hill to the left of the wash protects an excellent stand of saguaros. The trail continues along the side of the hill for a short distance before descending into a creek bed. For nearly a mile the trail follows the usually dry creek bed, crossing occasionally from one side to the other.

The trail leaves the creek and is now in the open. It is wide and sandy and is almost a road. Signs and sounds of civilization—telephone

Bowen House on the David Yetman Trail.

poles and the sound of automobiles—begin to appear. A sign indicates the direction of the David Yetman Trail. Continue to the left on the David Yetman Trail.

The Yetman Trail goes past the sign, to the left, along an old jeep road. The road drops into a wash and begins a gradual climb uphill. A trail sign indicates that the Yetman Trailhead turns to the left.

The trail now becomes narrow and soon parallels the fenced boundary of Tucson Mountain Park. The structure to the right and across the drainage is a storage facility for the Central Arizona Project. Also visible from this section of the trail are the downtown Tucson area and the Santa Catalina Mountains. There is an unusual number of young saguaros along the east side of the ridge, probably one hundred or more in the fifteen- to twenty-five-year-old range. The trail is narrow, has lots of loose rocks, and climbs rather steeply to the top of the ridge, where the other side of the mountain, including Gates Pass, is visible.

The Yetman Trail continues straight downhill. This is a very pleasant part of the trail. It goes gently downhill through a level valley. There is no sign of civilization here and it is very peaceful. There is an abundance of saguaro of all sizes. In early spring there is a scattering of golden Mexican poppies and other wildflowers in this valley. Small "Trail" signs indicate the correct route, which, at this point, drops into a creek bed, whose sandy bottom makes for more difficult walking.

A short way down the wash, a path leads to the left out of the wash to a stone house. The house has no roof, and the structure shows signs of fire damage; still the sturdy walls remain. The house was built in the early 1930s by Sherry Bowen, a typesetter and, later, city editor for the *Arizona Daily Star.* Sherry brought his wife, Ruby, to Tucson from Rockford, Illinois, in the late 1920s, hoping that the climate would help her serious heart condition. They first lived in Tucson, but soon homesteaded in the Tucson Mountains, eventually owning 2,000 acres. They moved to the homestead in 1931, living in a cabin while the house was being built.

Ruby Bowen kept a diary of her first year in the Tucson Mountains. She talks of the wild mountain sheep that came to the base of the cliffs to graze nearly every evening and then majestically climbed the steep canyon walls, to return to a cave that was their home. A mountain lion would pace about when Ruby was cooking meat and one time attempted to get in the window. Javelina, deer, and even a herd of wild horses came into their canyon.

The recuperative powers of the desert worked. The Bowens' daughter was born in 1943. They left Tucson in 1944 for New York City, where Sherry Bowen worked for the Associated Press. The valley and their homestead became part of Tucson Mountain Park in 1983.

The trail passes to the left of the house, crosses the creek, and again follows the creek bed, now wide and sandy. The trail follows the creek bed to the trailhead. On the left side of the creek there are hundreds of healthy saguaros. Unfortunately, many of the saguaros have been vandalized, cut at about the four-foot level. Many survived this vicious attack and now have several arms rising above the cuts. In early spring the creek bed is covered with an assortment of wildflowers. The trailhead marks the boundary of the Tucson Mountain Park. To reach your vehicle, you'll need to walk a little farther along on an unpaved road, through privately owned land, until you come to the Camino de Oeste parking lot.

Brown Mountain Trail

General Description: A ridge hike with spectacular views

Difficulty: Moderate, few areas of steep climbing

Best Time of Year to Hike: Winter, early spring, late fall

Length: 3.4 miles one way

Miles to Trailhead from Speedway/Campbell Intersection: 13.5 miles

Directions to Trailhead from Speedway/Campbell Intersection: Go west on Speedway, through Gates Pass to the intersection of Kinney Road. (Speedway becomes Gates Pass Road at Anklam Road.) Turn right on Kinney Road to Gilbert Ray Campground entrance (on McCain Loop Road) and turn left after 0.4 of a mile. The parking area for the trailhead is on the right and is signed. (The ideal way to hike this ridge is with two vehicles. Leave one at the Juan Santa Cruz Picnic Area 0.4 of a mile beyond the pull-in for the Gilbert Ray Campground, on the left, before the Arizona-Sonora Desert Museum.)

■ ■ ■

The Brown Mountain Trail is an interesting trek along a ridge in the heart of the Tucson Mountains. The ridge was named for Cornelius B. Brown, Pima County agricultural agent from 1920 to 1945, who was instrumental in the creation of Tucson Mountain Park in 1929. Brown is remembered as the "Father of Tucson Mountain Park."

The Brown Mountain Trail leaves from the southwest side of the parking area and crosses the desert to a deep wash. The trail continues across a smaller wash and after a rocky quarter of a mile, switchbacks up the mountain. For much of this hike you will be treated to a saguaro

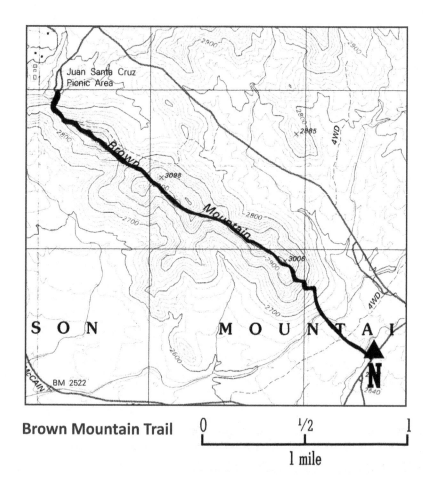

Brown Mountain Trail

0   ¹/2   1

1 mile

education. Saguaros in all stages of growth—from a few inches to over 20 feet tall to ribbed skeletons outlined against the sky—are along the trail.

A short elevation gain brings you to the top of the first peak. Look back for sweeping views to the east. Closest to you is Gilbert Ray Campground. During the winter months campers in every conceivable type of camping rig enjoy a respite from northern winters.

Notice the road winding down through Gates Pass to the base of Golden Gate Mountain. To the left of Gates Pass and high on the ridge are two houses that look like dollhouses from vantage point. These

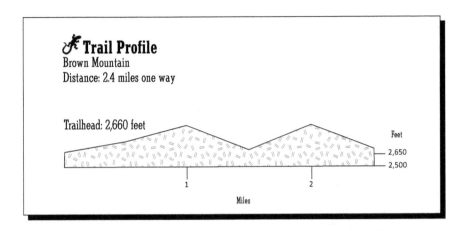

Trail Profile
Brown Mountain
Distance: 2.4 miles one way

Trailhead: 2,660 feet

Feet
2,650
2,500

Miles

homes were the scene of an environmental controversy in the late 1970s. The homes were built by partners in a construction firm, who were accused of flagrantly violating the community's wishes, by bull-dozing a road to the homesite just before the Pima County Board of Su-pervisors passed an ordinance preventing building on steep slopes and ridges. In 1977 vandals hot-wired a bulldozer and knocked down the walls of the houses, then under construction. The following year, both houses were damaged by fires of suspicious origin.

The controversy resurfaced late in 1986, when the owner of one of the homes requested permission to double the size of his house as well as add a guesthouse and heliport. After much debate, the Pima County Board of Supervisors approved the expansion of the house but denied permission for the guesthouse and heliport. The owner agreed to stabilize the road and add vegetation to help conceal the road lead-ing to the houses.

At the base of Golden Gate Mountain and to your right is a cluster of buildings that comprise Old Tucson Studios. Built in 1939 by Co-lumbia Pictures for the filming of *Arizona*, the first outdoor color West-ern movie, the set has been home to many Westerns over the years, such as *Gunfight at the O.K. Corral, Rio Bravo, Cimarron,* and *Three Ami-gos.* In later years the television series *Gunsmoke, High Chaparral,* and *Bonanza* were filmed at Old Tucson Studios. From 1989 until 1992, the television series *Young Riders* brought action to Old Tucson and its companion site at Mescal. Most of Old Tucson burned in a spectacular

Hiker checking saguaro cactus skeleton on Brown Mountain Trail.

fire in the summer of 1995. It has since been restored and welcomes guests from all over the world for tours and special events, such as Wild West Days.

The hike across Brown Mountain is noted for an abundance of saguaros of all sizes. From one spot I could count twenty small saguaros, not more than three feet tall. This is very unusual, because the area is not a protected one, normally thought capable of support-ing such a heavy growth of young cacti.

The trail crosses the ridge, going up and down and occasionally along the side of the mountain. The views are always excellent. Several great lookout spots provide views of the western valley, where Babo-quivari and Kitt Peaks are the dominant landmarks. To the southwest, you can trace the canal of the Central Arizona Project. Closer in is the Arizona-Sonora Desert Museum,

As you come to the end of the ridge, the trail switchbacks sharply down to the Juan Santa Cruz Picnic Area, where, if you have a vehicle waiting, you hop in and drive back to the trailhead. If not, it's back up the ridge and back to the parking area near the Gilbert Ray Campground.

Cam-Boh–Ironwood Forest–Picture Rocks Wash–Ringtail Loop

General Description: A meandering loop through abundant stands of saguaro and ironwood trees that begins and ends on Picture Rocks Road

Difficulty: Easy

Best Time of Year to Hike: Late fall, winter, early spring

Length: 3.5 mile loop

Miles to Trailhead from Speedway/Campbell Intersection: 18.8 miles

Directions to Trailhead from Speedway/Campbell Intersection: Go west on Speedway to Main. Turn right. Main becomes Oracle Road. Follow Oracle Road to Ina Road. Turn left on Ina Road. Ina Road continues under Interstate 10 and becomes North Wade Road at a sharp left turn just past Cortaro Road. North Wade Road becomes Picture Rocks Road before crossing the pass. As you descend the pass look for a large paved parking area on the right. Park here to access the Cam–Boh–Ironwood Forest–Picture Rocks Wash–Ringtail Loop. The loop begins in the wash directly across the road. THIS IS A HEAVILY TRAVELED ROAD. CROSS CAREFULLY.

Fees: Entrance to Saguaro National Park is $10 for any privately owned vehicle or motorcycle and $5 for any individual on foot or bicycle. Entry is valid for seven days. Several passes are also available: Saguaro National Park Annual Pass, $25, is valid for one year from the date of purchase; America the Beautiful Annual Pass, $80; America the Beautiful, Senior

Pass, $10, is a lifetime pass to National Park and Recreation Areas for US citizens age 62 and over; and the Access Pass, a lifetime pass for US citizens or permanent residents with permanent disabilities. Passes may be purchased at the Saguaro National Park Visitor Centers.

■ ■ ■

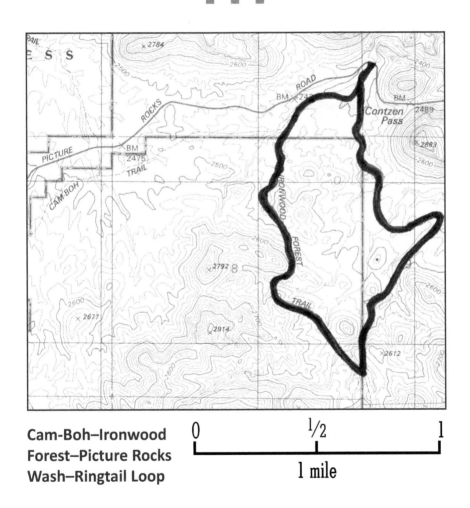

Cam-Boh–Ironwood Forest–Picture Rocks Wash–Ringtail Loop

0   ½   1

1 mile

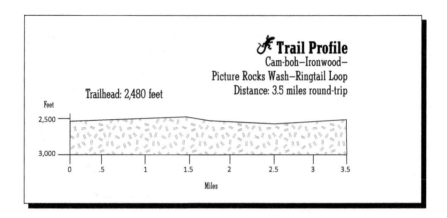

Despite the distance to the trailhead and the somewhat awkward combination of four trails, the Cam-Boh–Ironwood Forest–Picture Rocks Wash–Ringtail Loop hike in the Tucson Mountains is well worth the effort. Take a map with you and enjoy the Sonoran Desert at its best.

After you cross the road and enter the wash, turn right on the Cam-Boh Trail, which is not signed at this point. In 0.4 mile a trail sign indicates that the Cam-Boh Trail continues straight ahead for 2.3 miles to a picnic area. Your route is to turn left on the Ironwood Forest Trail, so named because of the abundance of ironwood trees that flourish in this area.

Ironwood trees are more like a large bush than a tree. In early spring, its many branches are covered with purplish blossoms. The blossoms become bean pods that provide food for desert animals. The dark, smooth wood of the ironwood tree is used by the Seri Indians of Sonora, Mexico, to make incredible carvings. The wood is also suitable for knife handles. In June of 2000 nearly 129,000 acres northwest of Tucson were designated as the Ironwood Forest National Monument by Presidential Proclamation to protect the ironwood trees and other desert vegetation.

As you climb to the high point of the Ironwood Forest Trail take time to look around. To the north you can see the cliffs of Panther and Safford Peaks. Wasson Peak stands out to the south.

Hiker examining an ironwood tree.

Notice the large number of small saguaros scattered among large saguaros with many arms. The saguaro is significant in the history of Arizona. The 1864 version of the Arizona Territorial Seal featured a saguaro. On March 16, 1901, the saguaro blossom was named the official territorial flower. The *Arizona Blue Book*—1929 to 1930—stated, "The pure white waxy flower of the Cereum Giganteus (Giant cactus) of Sahuara shall be the state flower of Arizona." The current law, as stated in Arizona Revised Statues, uses the current spelling, saguaro.

As you begin to go slightly downhill, look for the intersection of the Ironwood Forest Trail and Picture Rocks Wash. Turn left on Picture Rocks Wash. The wash is named for petroglyphs on the cliffs of the wash, most likely drawn by the Hohokam people who lived in this area in prehistoric times. Watch carefully on the left as you begin walking down the wash for petroglyphs depicting a human hand and a large bird. Bring binoculars to help spot petroglyphs higher on the side of the cliffs.

Watch on the left for the junction of the Ringtail Trail. This is the route back to your vehicle. At first, it appears that you are headed in the wrong direction, but you aren't. The trail soon bears to the right and heads for Picture Rocks Road.

Your chances of spotting a ringtail are greater if you are hiking in the evening. The name "ringtail" comes from the seven to eight rings around its tail. Although the ringtail is about the size of an adult cat, it is not related to the cat family, but is a member of the raccoon family. The ringtail is the state mammal of Arizona.

Cross the road carefully to return to your vehicle.

THE
RINCON
MOUNTAINS

Rincón means corner in Spanish. Topped by the 8,666-foot Mica Mountain, the Rincons have historically been the least accessible of the four ranges around Tucson.

Hohokam Indians camped and lived in the Rincons, as they did in the Santa Catalina and the Tucson Mountains. In Box Canyon, five bedrock mortars show where Indian women ground legumes. Petroglyphs adorn rocks and cliffs. When the Hohokam left, the mountains were generally free of human habitation until the early 1800s, when the Apache Indians wandered into the range. The mining that led to the development of the other ranges was almost nonexistent in the Rincons.

By the late 1800s the lower areas of the Rincons saw extensive ranching. The Tanque Verde Guest Ranch at the end of Speedway was once the ranch of Emilio Carrillo. Carrillo's and other ranchers' cattle grazed in the foothills of the Rincons, trampling small saguaros. Lime kilns that were operated in the 1880s used twelve cords of wood at each firing, the gathering of which seriously deforested the area. The remains of these kilns can be seen along the Cactus Forest Trail.

The Rincons were as cool and attractive as the Santa Catalinas, but few people took advantage of their heights. One who did was Levi Manning, a mayor of Tucson and former surveyor general of the United States. He discovered a flat area at about 8,000 feet near Mica Mountain and decided to homestead the area. In preparation for this, he had Mexican laborers build a wagon road to the site, and he constructed a large log cabin. For a few years Manning Camp was the social center of Tucson in the summer months. He even hauled a piano to the site. However, his homestead application had not been approved when the Rincon

Mountains became part of the Coronado National Forest, and it was declared void. Manning abandoned the camp and never returned.

The Forest Service began using the cabin and the site in the early 1920s to set up a permanent fire-control center. The camp has been spruced up with modern conveniences and additional bunkhouses over the years. Maintaining the camp became too expensive, and in 1976 everything was dismantled except the original log cabin, which Manning built in the early 1900s. That cabin is still used by the staff of the Saguaro National Park when they are working in the area.

The foothills of the Rincons drew the attention of world-renowned ecologist and University of Arizona president Homer Shantz in the late 1920s. Shantz dreamed of preserving the magnificent stand of saguaros for use as a study area. Through his efforts the state did purchase the land, but when the depression hit, the state was unable to keep up the payments. Through a property transfer agreement, the federal government took over in 1933, establishing the Saguaro National Monument. Additional property was purchased from private individuals in the early 1970s.

In 1939, a few years after the establishment of the monument, great numbers of the giant saguaros began to rot and die. Coincidentally, in February of that year the coldest temperatures ever recorded caused the mercury to fall to 25 degrees Fahrenheit and remain there for several hours. At first, plant scientists did not make any connection between the low temperatures and the diseased plants. By 1941, so many saguaros were dying that the National Park Service (NPS) removed diseased arms and buried whole plants that showed evidence of the rot. Plans were considered for transplanting young saguaros in the area. Before this was implemented, the policy of the National Park Service had become more accepting of nature and did not interfere with the natural progression of plant life.

In the two decades that followed, extensive studies were conducted on the saguaro population. The studies led scientists to conclude that the freeze of 1939 had weakened the old giant saguaros by making them susceptible to the bacterial infection, and that the demise of the saguaros was just part of the natural cycle in their long lives. Younger, stronger plants are able to fight off infection by forming a "boot," or callus, and sealing off the disease from the rest of the plant.

An attack of a different kind occurred in the mid-1950s. The National Park Service drew up plans to develop the Rincon Mountains in a manner similar to the Mount Lemmon area. NPS planned to build a nineteen-mile road called the Desert Mountain Highway from the monument headquarters to Manning Camp. The thinking at the time was that such development would relieve the stress on the Mount Lemmon area and that the rapid growth of the Tucson area demanded more recreational facilities. Fortunately for hikers who enjoy the wilderness, the Desert Mountain Highway never materialized.

In 1994, the status of the Saguaro National Monument changed, and today it is known as Saguaro National Park. Because this guide is restricted to hikes that can be completed in one day, I have included only six hikes in the Rincon Mountains. One is an exceptionally easy trek along the Cactus Forest Trail. A moderate hike goes from the Broadway Trailhead to Garwood Dam. The Douglas Spring and Tanque Verde Ridge Trails are long but relatively easy hikes across the foothills to about the 6,000-foot level. A new section of the Arizona Trail known as the Quilter Trail has recently opened. The only hike I have included that gets you into the high country is the hike to Rincon Peak.

Cactus Forest Trail

General Description: A basically flat ramble across the desert, through many varieties of cacti and past some old lime kilns

Difficulty: Easy

Best Time of Year to Hike: Winter, late fall, early spring

Length: 10.4 miles round-trip

Miles to Trailhead from Speedway/Campbell Intersection: 13.9 miles

Directions to Trailhead from Speedway/Campbell Intersection: Go south on Campbell to the intersection of Broadway. Turn east (left) on Broadway, following it until a sign indicates 1.5 miles to the dead end of Broadway. About 0.2 mile beyond the sign, a parking area on the right indicates the beginning of Cactus Forest Trail.

Fees: Entrance to Saguaro National Park is $10 for any privately owned vehicle or motorcycle and $5 for any individual on foot or bicycle. Entry is valid for seven days. Several passes are also available: Saguaro National Park Annual Pass, $25, is valid for one year from the date of purchase; America the Beautiful Annual Pass, $80; America the Beautiful, Senior Pass, $10, is a lifetime pass to National Park and Recreation Areas for US citizens age 62 and over; and the Access Pass, a lifetime pass for US citizens or permanent residents with permanent disabilities. Passes may be purchased at the Saguaro National Park Visitor Centers.

■　■　■

The Cactus Forest Trail meanders across the desert from Broadway Boulevard to Old Spanish Trail and is a good introduction to the

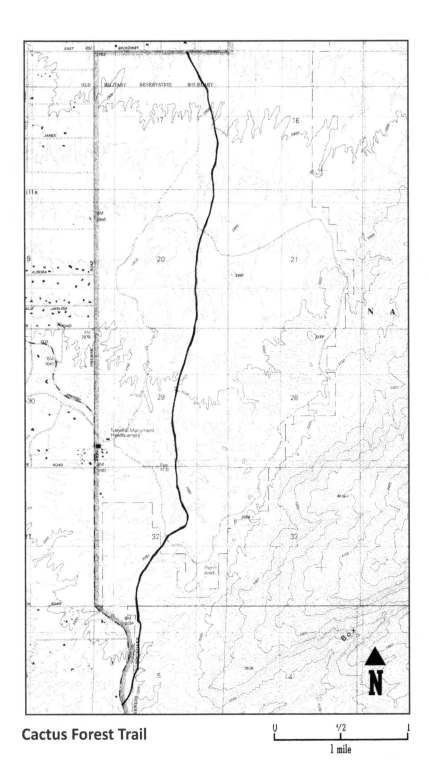

Cactus Forest Trail

0 .... 1/2 1

1 mile

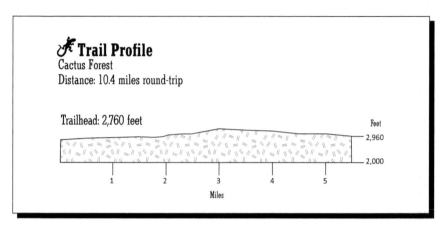

⚘ Trail Profile

Cactus Forest

Distance: 10.4 miles round-trip

Trailhead: 2,760 feet

lowlands of the Rincon Mountains. The ideal way to hike this trail is to leave a vehicle at the trailhead parking area on Old Spanish Trail and begin the hike from the Broadway trailhead.

I recommend stopping at the Saguaro National Park East Visitor Center at the intersection of Freeman Road and Old Spanish Trail to pick up the brochure showing the Cactus Forest Trail System before hiking this trail. A small trail sign marks the beginning of the Cactus Forest Trail. Follow the arrow to the left 0.1 mile to the intersection of the Shantz Trail. Again, follow the arrow pointing in the direction of the Cactus Forest Trail.

The smooth, sandy trail passes many old, giant saguaros. Although palo verde and mesquite trees "nurse" a number of young saguaros here, this area is primarily an aging saguaro forest. The saguaro and an abundance of other cactus varieties make the name Cactus Forest Trail appropriate.

For most of the trail there is little elevation gain or loss. Mostly level, the trail drops in and out of several small drainages and occasionally crosses a sandy wash. At 0.7 of a mile a sign indicates the intersection of the Cholla Trail. If you want a brief look at this area, the Cholla Trail makes a 2.1-mile loop with the Loma Verde/Mesa Trails and rejoins the Cactus Forest Trail. To stay on the main Cactus Forest Trail, continue straight ahead. This section has many creosote bushes. If you rub a few leaves and smell your fingers, you will realize why it is called creosote, even though the plant has no connection with the actual substance. In early spring the tiny yellow flowers of the creosote bush make a showy display.

Lime kilns first used in the 1880s, Cactus Forest Trail.

You will note that there are several side trails leading off the main trail. Always continue straight ahead, avoiding any side trails. As you hike this trail, see how many small saguaro you can spot. Because this area was heavily grazed in earlier years, there are very few remaining small saguaro. It will take well over one hundred years before this may once again be a "cactus forest."

As you approach the paved road of Saguaro National Park East, you see a small hill to the left called Observatory Hill. When this area was owned by the University of Arizona, there was some discussion about building an observatory on this hill and the top was leveled, but the property was acquired by the federal government before any such plans materialized. Beside the drive is a sign for the Cactus Forest trailhead, at which point you will have come 1.8 miles. Cross the road in the painted crosswalk and continue the trail on the other side. Bicycles are permitted on this section between the paved road segments. In a few hundred yards you pass some concrete foundations on the right. This was the location of the park's first ranger station.

Nine-tenths of a mile from Cactus Forest Drive are the lime kilns, large beehive structures to the left and below the trail. A sign explains that these kilns were constructed around 1880. Limestone was brought down from the nearby hills and heated to a very high temperature to form lime. The lime was used to produce mortar and whitewash. Each batch of lime burned about twelve cords of wood from nearby trees. Carmen Moreno operated the kilns from 1914 to 1917, selling lime to Tucson building contractors for $10 a ton. This lime was used in the construction of the rock wall around the University of Arizona. In 1920, ranchers forced the closure of the kilns because of the destruction of cattle forage. A warning that bee colonies now inhabit the kilns is not needed, because the bees themselves prohibit close inspection of the kilns. Also, once, when I leaned over to take a picture of one of the kilns, a huge rattler encouraged me on my way! The kilns are an important part of the history of this area and should be left undisturbed.

Right past the kilns is a sign that says, "Dead End Trail." This is an easy 0.4-mile jaunt to Lime Falls. Thinking that I would find a waterfall, I took the side trip. Although the trail does drop into a large wash and through a thick mesquite forest, my hope of finding water was not realized. It is a pretty area, however, and at the correct time of day, as evidenced by the large number of deer and javelina footprints, your chances of seeing wildlife would be excellent.

Past the dead-end trail sign, the Cactus Forest Trail goes through an area with very few cacti. A low gray-green shrub and short grasses predominate. Here the trail begins to climb slightly for the first time, going up and down a series of small hills, making a nice change. The sweeping views of the surrounding mountain ranges are dramatic.

As the trail nears West Cactus Forest Drive, there are many side trails that can be confusing, again as a result of the large number of horseback riders in the area. Continue straight ahead. The trail is wide and sandy at this point. To the left is a large wash that has cut quite a swath in times of heavy runoff. There are many large mesquite trees. It is in this area that the great horned owls breed. The trail becomes an old road in this area, and again there are very few cacti, just a few prickly pears and chollas.

The trail crosses West Cactus Forest Drive and continues 0.9 of a mile to Old Spanish Trail. This portion of the trail is rarely used and the trail is not well maintained. Hopefully you will have left a vehicle in the parking area. Otherwise, it's 5.2 miles back to the Broadway Trailhead.

Broadway Trailhead
to Garwood Dam

General Description: A pleasant hike across the desert to a large dam

Difficulty: Moderate

Best Time of Year to Hike: Winter, early spring, late fall

Length: 5.4 miles round-trip

Miles to Trailhead from Speedway/Campbell Intersection: 13.9 miles

Directions to Trailhead from Speedway/Campbell Intersection: Go south on Campbell to the intersection of Broadway Boulevard. Turn east (left) on Broadway, following it until a sign indicates 1.5 miles to the dead end of Broadway. About 0.2 mile beyond the sign, a parking area on the left is signed as the Broadway Trailhead. The route to Pink Hill and Garwood Dam begins across the road. A large sign to the left of the trailhead depicts the trails in the area. Sign in at the register before beginning the hike.

Fees: Entrance to Saguaro National Park is $10 for any privately owned vehicle or motorcycle and $5 for any individual on foot or bicycle. Entry is valid for seven days. Several passes are also available: Saguaro National Park Annual Pass, $25, is valid for one year from the date of purchase; America the Beautiful Annual Pass, $80; America the Beautiful, Senior Pass, $10, is a lifetime pass to National Park and Recreation Areas for US citizens age 62 and over; and the Access Pass, a lifetime pass for US citizens or permanent residents with permanent disabilities. Passes may be purchased at the Saguaro National Park Visitor Centers.

■ ▥ ▦

Hiking from the Broadway Trailhead past Pink Hill to Garwood Dam requires careful attention to the trail signs. Detailed maps are available at Saguaro National Park (Rincon Mountain District - East) Visitor Center on Old Spanish Trail and at local outdoor stores. A large sign at the trailhead depicts the trails in the area.

From the trailhead, turn left, following the Shantz Trail for 0.1 mile to the intersection of the Shantz Trail and the Cactus Forest Trail. Continue on the Shantz Trail, following the arrow to the Pink Hill Trail. As you stand facing the sign for the Pink Hill Trail notice that "Pink Hill Trail" is written at the top of the sign and does not have a directional arrow. This indicates that the Pink Hill Trail is straight ahead.

Let's hope you are not already confused! Here's the scenario. You've turned left at the trailhead, turned left on the Shantz Trail, and are hiking along on the Shantz Trail, when you come to the intersection of the Pink Hill Trail. Now turn right on the Pink Hill Trail, toward the Rincon Mountains to the east. Voilà! The Pink Hill Trail crosses Javelina Wash before coming to the Loma Verde Wash, a deeper, more pronounced wash. Just past the Loma Verde Wash, a trail intersection sign marks the meeting of the Loma Verde and Pink Hill Trails.

Follow the Pink Hill Trail straight ahead toward the mountains. It crosses Monument Wash before circling Pink Hill. Steps lead to the top of Pink Hill. Climb it now or on your return from Garwood Dam. There

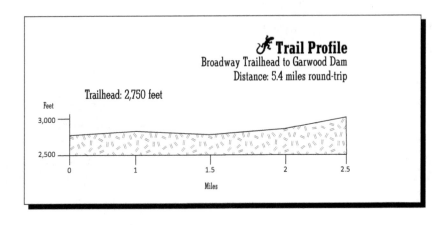

🦎 **Trail Profile**
Broadway Trailhead to Garwood Dam
Distance: 5.4 miles round-trip

Trailhead: 2,750 feet

Feet

3,000 —

2,500 —

0   1   1.5   2   2.5

Miles

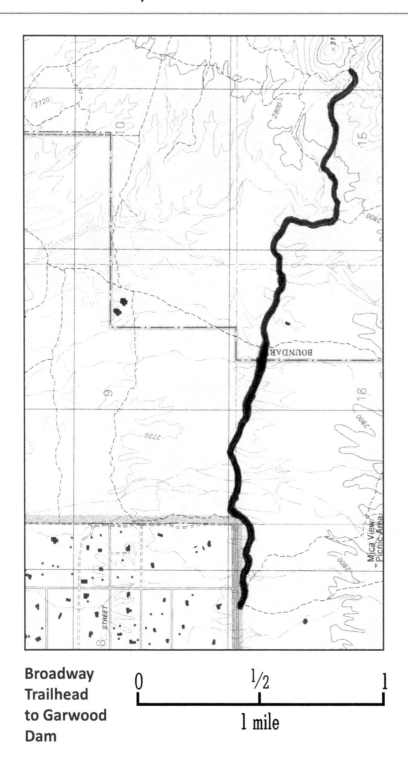

Broadway Trailhead to Garwood Dam

0   1/2   1

1 mile

Garwood Dam.

are excellent views from the top of Pink Hill of the Santa Catalina and Tucson Mountains and most of the city of Tucson. As you look directly east toward the Rincons, you can see Wild Horse Canyon and the old wagon road climbing the side of the mountain into the canyon.

To reach Garwood Dam turn right on Squeeze Pen Trail. For 0.3 of a mile you will head south, parallel to the Rincons. When you reach the Carrillo Trail intersection, turn left, and you are again heading up the mountain. The Carrillo Trail meanders along the side of a large drainage, which is the drainage out of Wild Horse Canyon. In early spring this is a good place to find wildflowers. After a few steps you get your first view of Garwood Dam.

The dam is a large concrete structure that crosses the lower portion of Wild Horse Canyon. It is slightly to the right and across the base of the mountain. Nelson Garwood, a rancher, built this dam as a water supply in the 1940s. He used a small room at the base of the dam to store equipment. Garwood's house was located on a flat area near the dam.

When you reach the intersection of the Garwood Trail, turn right on the old wagon road that leads to Garwood Dam. This is still the Carrillo Trail. As you round the curve in the road, look below on the right. There are large pools of water and most of the year there is some water flowing. When you reach the dam, you will be surprised at the size of the structure. It is tempting, but unsafe, to walk across the dam but you can relax and sit on the edge of the dam.

Take a moment and look toward the Broadway Trailhead. You will see a small hill that, in the right light, has a pink tint. This is Pink Hill.

Tanque Verde Ridge Trail

General Description: A hike along the ridgeline through changing vegetation to the Juniper Basin Campground

Difficulty: Difficult, some areas of steep climbing

Best Time of Year to Hike: Winter, early spring, late fall

Length: 13.8 miles round-trip

Miles to Trailhead from Speedway/Campbell Intersection: 11.5 miles to Visitor Center parking lot; 1 mile to Javelina Picnic Area

Directions to Trailhead from Speedway/Campbell Intersection: Go south on Campbell to the intersection of Broadway Boulevard. Turn east (left) on Broadway until the intersection of Old Spanish Trail. There is no light at this intersection. It is past the intersection of Pantano Road and before Camino Seco. Turn right on Old Spanish Trail to the entrance of Saguaro National Park East District. Enter the park and follow signs to the Javelina Picnic Area. A sign indicates the parking area for the Tanque Verde Ridge Trail.

Fees: Entrance to Saguaro National Park is $10 for any privately owned vehicle or motorcycle and $5 for any individual on foot or bicycle. Entry is valid for seven days. Several passes are also available: Saguaro National Park Annual Pass, $25, is valid for one year from the date of purchase; America the Beautiful Annual Pass, $80; America the Beautiful, Senior Pass, $10, is a lifetime pass to National Park and Recreation Areas for US citizens age 62 and over; and the Access Pass, a lifetime pass for US citizens or permanent residents with permanent disabilities. Passes may be purchased at the Saguaro National Park Visitor Centers.

■ ■ ■

T*anque verde*, Spanish for "green tank," is a name used often in the Rincon Mountains. There's a Tanque Verde wash, falls, canyon, ridge, peak, guest ranch, and, of course, hiking trail. Its use originated in the 1860s, when rancher William Oury tried to avoid Indian attacks on his cattle by moving the entire herd to the base of a ridge on the southeast corner of the Rincons. Two large water holes (or tanks) containing green algae were on the range, and the area came to be referred to as Tanque Verde.

The Tanque Verde Trail follows Tanque Verde Ridge to Juniper Basin and on to Cowhead Saddle, where it connects with the Cowhead Saddle Trail to continue the climb to Manning Camp. The section of the trail that ends at Juniper Basin makes an excellent, although long, day hike.

The trail begins to the right of the Javelina Picnic Area. It goes slightly downhill and crosses a small drainage, before beginning to climb. There are many cacti in this area, including several large, healthy saguaros. Past another small drainage is a trail register.

View of Tucson from the Tanque Verde Ridge Trail.

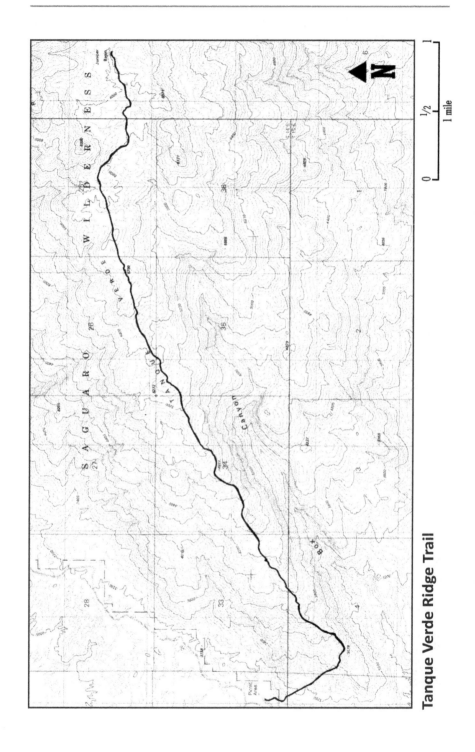

Tanque Verde Ridge Trail

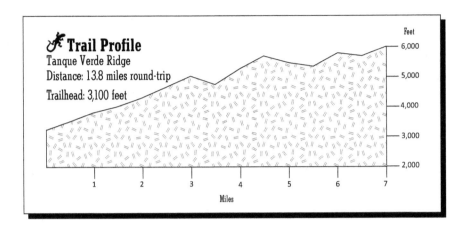

Trail Profile
Tanque Verde Ridge
Distance: 13.8 miles round-trip
Trailhead: 3,100 feet

After the trail register the climb is steeper, and you quickly come to a good lookout point, from which you can see the telescopes on Kitt Peak and most of the southern part of Tucson. After this lookout point, the trail levels out and is smooth and sandy for a short distance, before it drops into another drainage. As the trail climbs out of this drainage, the climb increases and the views get better. You can see all of Tucson and, on a clear day, as far north as Picacho Peak. Occasionally there is a faint side trail where hikers have gone for a better view, or the trail crosses rock slabs, making the correct route somewhat confusing. Take your time, look for cairns, and avoid stepping over a row of rocks intended to stop you from taking the wrong trail. For the most part, the Tanque Verde Ridge Trail is easy to follow, and if you do go astray momentarily, it is always possible to backtrack and find the correct route.

The first part of the trail follows a pattern of crossing small drainages and leveling out for awhile, with the views of the valley ever improving. After about 1.5 miles you top out on the ridge, and you can see why the name Tanque Verde Ridge Trail is justified. Most of the trail from here on follows the ridgeline, going to either the north or south, but always coming back to the ridge. The views from the ridge are spectacular. To the south in the Santa Ritas are Mount Wrightson and Mount Hopkins. Ahead and to the southeast is Rincon Peak. To the west are the Tucson Mountains, and to the north, a magnificent view of the Santa Catalinas.

The vegetation is typical of this elevation. Saguaro, prickly pear, cholla, ocotillo, and hedgehog make this area especially pretty in mid-April when the cacti bloom. As you leave the ridgeline and begin to circle the hill to the north, there is a deep drainage on the left. Along this section of the trail is a small sign that indicates that you have reached the 4,000-foot elevation level. Past the sign is a drainage that occasionally has small pools of water, especially after a summer rain. There are long stretches of flat, easy walking, with only slight elevation gain. Rarely do you find a shady spot. The views continue to be great, and this would be an excellent place to hike to see the sunset and then the lights of the city at night.

Past the 4,000-foot sign, the saguaros become scarce, and a few varieties of oak begin to appear. There is a large section covered with bear grass. Bear grass is used today by Tohono O'odham basket makers. Many years ago, the sharp-edged grass was used by the Apaches to cut off the noses of women accused of adultery.

An interesting feature of this hike is the opportunity to observe the changing vegetation that accompanies the increase in elevation. Past the section covered with bear grass, the first juniper and piñon pines begin to appear. The trail occasionally tops out on the ridge, levels out for a distance, and then drops to the north or south side of the ridge. The views are amazing, and this is one of the best parts of the Tanque Verde Trail, because it has views in all directions.

About two miles past the 4,000-foot marker, you come to another sign that indicates a 5,000-foot elevation. From here, it takes almost two hours to reach the campground. By now there are no saguaros. The vegetation is mainly several varieties of oak, juniper and piñon pine, and manzanita. The plant that I call the hiker's nemesis, amole, commonly known as shindaggers, begins to appear. Imagine how it would feel to tumble into a patch of amole!

You are now far back into the foothills of the Rincons, and the rest of the trail goes up and down small hills. As you progress into the foothills, the trees increase in density and size. As you continue along the trail, the city disappears, and the views are not as spectacular. You have the feeling of real isolation in this area.

After you drop into a narrow, sandy streambed, you are about a mile from the Juniper Basin Campground. For a few hundred yards, there is a section of loose rock that makes the climb more difficult. Red metal strips are now on the trees to mark the trail so that it can be followed in snow.

Soon the trail crosses a wide, flat, rocky area. Several large cairns mark the correct route. Across the rocks, the trail goes along the side of a drainage and is a pretty area. The trees are much larger now. You then cross a streambed, with an unusual dark gray rock bottom. A few hundred yards past this stream bed is the Juniper Basin Campground.

Reservations must be made at park headquarters for overnight camping. There are picnic tables, grills, and a rest room at the campground. The area is covered with exceptionally large juniper, the bark of which looks much like the skin of an alligator, thus, the common name of the tree is alligator juniper. The elevation at the campground is 6,000 feet.

Hiking time to the campground is four to five hours, with a little less time required for the return. Unless, that is, you happen to be carrying heavy backpacks, as did the three volunteer rangers we found camped at Juniper Basin on our last hike into this area. Rick Collins, Roger Carrillo, and Jeff Coleman were spending several days at the campground, doing trail and campground maintenance and removing pink tags left by an extensive search and rescue operation the previous summer. Should you be interested in becoming a volunteer ranger, stop by the Saguaro National Park East Visitor Center on your return for information. The "three Cs," as they call themselves, seemed to be enjoying their work and even invited us to stop by for dinner. But, alas, we couldn't accept. We had 6.9 miles to go before dark!

Douglas Spring Trail

General Description: A hike to Douglas Spring Campground, through an area recovering from a major fire in the summer of 1989

Difficulty: Difficult

Best Time of Year to Hike: Winter, early spring, late fall

Length: 11.8 miles round-trip

Miles to Trailhead from Speedway/Campbell Intersection: 15 miles

Directions to Trailhead from Speedway/Campbell Intersection: Follow Speedway Boulevard east until it ends at the trailhead.

Fees: Entrance to Saguaro National Park is $10 for any privately owned vehicle or motorcycle and $5 for any individual on foot or bicycle. Entry is valid for seven days. Several passes are also available: Saguaro National Park Annual Pass, $25, is valid for one year from the date of purchase; America the Beautiful Annual Pass, $80; America the Beautiful, Senior Pass, $10, is a lifetime pass to National Park and Recreation Areas for US citizens age 62 and over; and the Access Pass, a lifetime pass for US citizens or permanent residents with permanent disabilities. Passes may be purchased at the Saguaro National Park Visitor Centers.

■ ■ ■

The Douglas Spring Trail crosses the foothills of the Rincon Mountains to the Douglas Spring Campground. Past the campground the trail continues to Cowhead Saddle and serves as a connecting trail for several loops used by backpackers. Much of the vegetation on the last

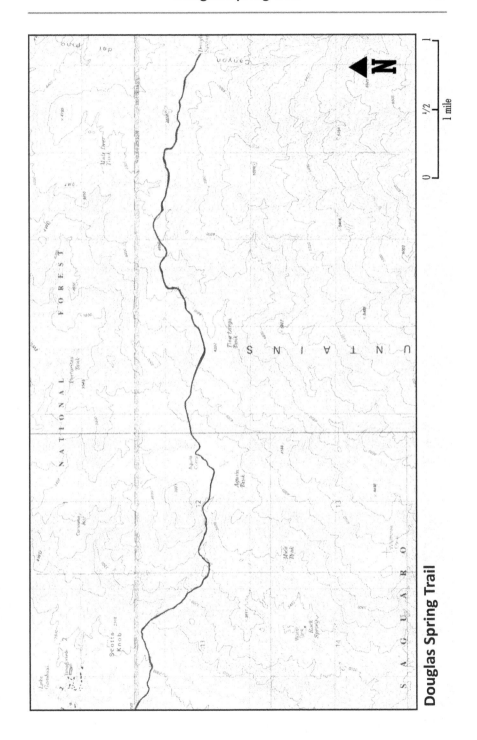

Douglas Spring Trail

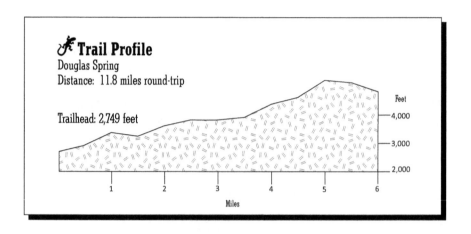

𝒻 **Trail Profile**
Douglas Spring
Distance: 11.8 miles round-trip

Trailhead: 2,749 feet

six miles of the trail was consumed by the Chiva Fire in the summer of 1989. Hiking this area today provides an example of the benefits of a fire. New growth covers most of the fire-damaged area.

A lightning strike on July 5, 1989, started a fire near the northern boundary of Saguaro National Park. The fire, which included the entire Douglas Spring Campground and much of the Douglas Spring Trail, burned 9,580 acres before it was controlled on July 10. After being closed for revegetation and rehabilitation for nearly ten months, the trail was reopened in April 1990. Today the trail is in excellent condition and is always easy to follow.

A sign at the trailhead describes the Manning Camp Trail system. This description will include that portion of the trail to Douglas Spring Campground. After 0.1 of a mile there is a trail register, and, as you can see by the number of signatures, this is a popular trail, especially on weekends. The first half mile of the trail is nearly level and passes through saguaro, prickly pear, barrel, and cholla cacti, ocotillo, and palo verde and mesquite trees. You will notice that there are very few small saguaros. Before becoming a preserved area, this section was heavily used by ranchers, and many small saguaros were trampled by cattle.

After the first half mile, the trail begins to climb gradually, and as you ascend, you see the buildings of the Tanque Verde Guest Ranch to the northeast and most of the Tucson Valley. The Douglas Spring Trail goes to the left of the hill and begins to climb more steeply. To the left of the trail is a deep, rugged drainage. Most of the year there are pools

Hikers starting up the beautiful Douglas Spring Trail.

of water and some water trickling over the rocks, making this an excellent spot to see wildlife, especially mule deer. As the trail climbs steeply around the hill, you will note that steps have been dug into the steeper sections, with rocks placed for erosion control. As you top the first hill, you come to a flat spot that is used frequently as a rest stop. You can see a trail beaten out to the top of the hill by hikers who wanted to see the view. There is no rush to do this, because there are several good viewing spots along the trail farther along.

There are many prickly pears along this trail. You may be surprised to learn that this common desert plant played an important part in world history. Look carefully on the prickly pear pads for a whitish, flaky substance that looks like artificial snow. This is actually a small insect—cochineal—that is the source of a brilliant red dye. When the Spanish explorer Hernán Cortés entered Mexico in 1519, he encountered Aztec men and women wearing dazzling red garments. On learning the source of the dye, Cortés arranged for prickly pear to be cultivated in Spain. For nearly three centuries, this was a closely guarded Spanish secret, so much so that the red cloth made from the dye became known as the "color of kings." Scrape a patch of cochineal with a stick and its tip will turn red, the color of kings.

From the flat spot the trail again begins to climb up the side of another hill, and by now the views of the city are excellent. Again there are good views of the drainage on the left. The trail continues to climb and switchback up the hill, flattens out for a short period, and then begins climbing again, this time along the right side of the hill. As you walk along the side of the hill, you'll see another drainage to the right. This frequently has water and is also a good spot to see wildlife. When I hiked this trail in early May I saw seven deer in this section. The trail climbs steeply for a short distance then once again levels out, continuing to follow the drainage.

From this point on, fire damage was extensive. When I hiked this trail in April 1990, prickly pears lay in heaps of discarded charcoal, ocotillo stalks looked like burned hot dog–roasting sticks, and many tall saguaros were blackened skeletons. Today, the recovery is remarkable. Tall native grasses cover the ground, and, if you didn't know it, you could never tell this area had been burned.

The trail crosses several small drainages but continues to follow to the left of the main drainage for a quarter mile, before turning away and gradually climbing another small hill and then traversing a long flat area. In this flat area you have good views of the inner foothills. Large drainages come down. At the intersection of the Three Tank Trail, note that there are 3.6 miles to go before reaching the Douglas Spring Campground.

There are several small drainages before crossing a wide, sandy drainage that comes down from a steep, rocky section known as Bridal Wreath Falls. The tall, green mesquite trees in the low basin below the falls were totally missed by the fire. A side trail leads off to the right, and you might like to take time and explore this green area and the falls. It is especially beautiful in early spring, when snowmelt creates a large waterfall. Just past the turnoff to Bridal Wreath Falls, there is a turnoff to the left to Ernie's Falls. Both trails are short and well worth exploring.

Past this green area the trail begins to climb again, this time quite steeply, before rounding a knoll and continuing to follow the drainage, which is by now a wide, sandy creek. In the drainage is what remains of a human-made wall. This is noted on the map as "Tina Larga Tank," and it contained water until being destroyed in the heavy rains of 1983.

As you continue to climb, the higher elevations of the Rincons stand out. The large outcropping of rocks straight ahead is Helen's Dome. A little farther east is Spud Rock, so named because a man of German descent retired from the railroad about 1890, moved into the Rincon Mountains, and raised potatoes near the rock.

After leaving the side of the hill, the trail rounds the hill, and you now begin a gradual decline into the Douglas Spring Campground, crossing in and out of several drainages, going up and down small hills, until reaching the campground. It is in this area that the fire was most intense, and where today, the damage is still most evident.

The campground, once an oasis of picnic tables and tall shade trees, is now composed of a rest room and signs indicating campsites. A few trees escaped the fire, but most of the shade is gone. There is still a spring, and water trickles over the rocks in the driest of seasons. If you've never been here before, you'll appreciate the solitude and enjoy watching birds fly among the dead trees—but if you remember the Douglas Spring Campground from before the fire, it's still too soon to go back. Give it another fifty years!

Rincon Peak Trail

General Description: One of the most beautiful and difficult trails in the Rincon Mountains

Difficulty: Extremely difficult

Best Time of Year to Hike: Late spring, early fall, summer

Length: 16.4 miles round-trip, via Miller Creek Trail

Miles to Trailhead from Speedway/Campbell Intersection: 57 miles

Directions to Trailhead from Speedway/Campbell Intersection: Go west on Speedway to I-10. Follow I-10 east to the Mescal Exit (297). Turn left on Mescal Road for 16 miles. The first 3 miles of Mescal Road is paved. The rest, including Forest Service (FS) roads, are unpaved but are suitable for passenger cars. En route you will pass Old Tucson Studios Mescal location on the left. Mescal Road becomes FS Road 35. At the intersection of FS 35 and FS 4407, a sign indicates that the Miller Creek trailhead is to the left. The trailhead is 0.2 of a mile from the sign.

Fees: Entrance to Saguaro National Park is $10 for any privately owned vehicle or motorcycle and $5 for any individual on foot or bicycle. Entry is valid for seven days. Several passes are also available: Saguaro National Park Annual Pass, $25, is valid for one year from the date of purchase; America the Beautiful Annual Pass, $80; America the Beautiful, Senior Pass, $10, is a lifetime pass to National Park and Recreation Areas for US citizens age 62 and over; and the Access Pass, a lifetime pass for US citizens or permanent residents with permanent disabilities. Passes may be purchased at the Saguaro National Park Visitor Centers.

■   ■   ■

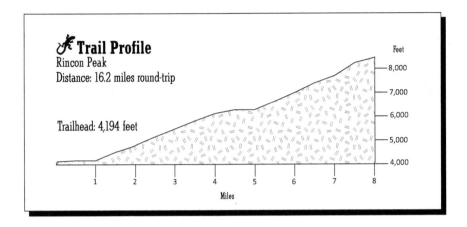

R incon Peak, at 8,482 feet, is the second highest peak in the Rincon Mountains. The Miller Creek Trail, in combination with the Rincon Peak Trail, is the shortest route (8.1 miles) to the summit. Although the Rincon Peak Trail is included in this guide as a day hike, one must be an exceptionally strong hiker to conquer this mountain in one day. If you plan to do so, I recommend that you drive to the trailhead the night before and begin your hike at daybreak.

The trail begins through a gate in the fence near the parking area. Markers indicate that this is part of the Arizona Trail System. The first part of the trail is level, crossing and recrossing Miller Creek several times. Most of the year there will be water in the stream and the resultant vegetation makes for a pretty area. The sandy trail passes under large Arizona sycamores and Emory oaks and through manzanita. There are a few large barrel cacti that look out of place among this vegetation. Grapevines grow high in many of the trees.

After about three-quarters of a mile you come to a large pool and a jumble of rocks. Here you cross Miller Creek and then go to the left of a small drainage. The trail then begins to climb gradually, leaving the drainage and veering to the right, climbing more steeply for 200 yards, before dropping again into and crossing another drainage.

Immediately across this drainage is a fence and signs marking the boundary of Saguaro National Park. There is a walk-through opening in the fence. The trail goes through a thick stand of manzanita, is sandy and rocky, and goes down and crosses a big boulder-strewn drainage.

Across the drainage, the trail climbs steeply with occasional level spots through a "boulder forest." Although there will be some pleasant, level stretches, the easy part of this trail is over. The trail is steep, with some high step-ups over the boulders. A misstep, such as the one I experienced on my last climb in the spring of 2011, can result in a nasty fall.

After a seemingly endless climb through the manzanita and around boulders of all sizes, the trail turns left and descends into an exceptionally beautiful area. The now level trail is covered by a canopy

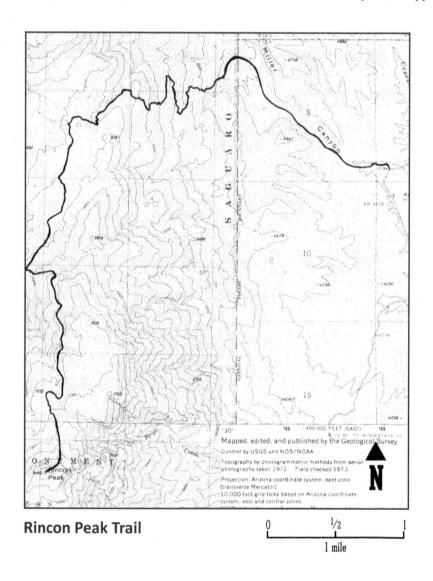

Rincon Peak Trail

0   1/2   1

1 mile

*Backpackers headed up Rincon Peak
to Happy Valley Campground.*

of trees. Much of the year water flows in this area. Near the head of the drainage is a ponderosa pine, the first of many to come. Past the ponderosa, the trail turns to the right and crosses a small drainage, before turning left. Here you begin to climb steeply again. The canopy is gone as the view opens up and the trail approaches Happy Valley Saddle. At the saddle you get a good view of your goal, Rincon Peak. It really doesn't look possible that you can be on top of this mountain in a few miles.

At the saddle the trail drops slightly to the intersection of the Miller Creek Trail and the Heartbreak Ridge Trail. Turn left at this intersection a half of a mile to the Rincon Peak Trail sign. Here you will turn left for the final climb to the top of Rincon Peak. An interesting side trip and an excellent spot for camping, should you decide to do this hike as a backpack, is to continue a half mile past the Rincon Peak Trail intersection, to Happy Valley Campground. The campground has four sites. Reservations must be made at Saguaro National Park East. There

*Hiker sitting on the area's largest cairn
on the summit of Rincon Peak.*

are grills, rest room facilities, and metal containers for storage of food. Tall ponderosas shade the area and carpet the ground with needles.

We'll assume that you are doing this trail as an all-out day effort and continue 3.3 miles up the Rincon Peak Trail to the summit. Past the intersection, the trail climbs slightly and then levels off. For nearly a mile the trail drops into and out of a series of small ravines. There are many alligator junipers and the ever-present manzanitas. The trail is still pleasant, and you may wonder where the difficult part is—don't worry, it will come soon enough. As the trail begins to climb, it crosses one large side drainage and, shortly, another one. By now you are in the open, where the views are astounding. Walk past a particularly thick stand of manzanitas and you can see the western end of Tucson. As you climb, more of the city will be visible. Past this point the trail begins to climb more steeply, with occasional switchbacks and some long, steep climbs. The views are always excellent. As you look toward Tucson, you can see Tanque Verde Ridge and catch a glimpse of the Santa Catalina Mountains.

The trail drops in and out of several deep ravines. By now you are in ponderosa country. Along the side of the mountain you come to a small spring. A circle of rocks contains the actual spring, and the area surrounding the spring is covered with tiny, green cloverlike plants. Past the spring you see the first Douglas fir. This is a beautiful section, not too steep, under a canopy of ponderosa pine and Douglas fir trees. The trail is soft and the climb imperceptible for a short distance. This cannot last if you are to reach the top.

Less than a mile from the summit, you reach a sign that says, "Foot Trail Only, No Stock." This sign marks the beginning of the final ascent on the peak. Be consoled by the spectacular views as you stop to rest. The trail is steep. There are some switchbacks, but not enough for my liking. A small patch of aspen trees grows near the top.

The top is worth the climb, and on a clear day, you can truly see forever. It takes the average hiker two to three hours to do the final 3.3 miles. Not much grows on the top. A few manzanitas and, surprisingly, a number of hedgehog cacti. The wind can be very strong. A cairn that is at least ten feet high marks the actual summit. A summit register is anchored in a metal box near the summit. Add your name to the list. Should there be any sign of a storm, get off the summit. As you can imagine, this is a target for lightning. Hopefully you can remain here for a while and, with the aid of a map, pick out the mountain ranges you can see from the summit. If you are doing this as a day hike, don't linger too long. The way down is treacherous and takes almost as long as it did to come up.

Quilter Trail

General Description: A newly opened section of the Arizona Trail, the Quilter Trail, crosses one of the most spectacular stands of saguaro in the Tucson area and provides stunning views of the surrounding area

Difficulty: Difficult

Best Time of Year to Hike: Early spring, winter, late fall

Length: 6.9 miles one way

Miles to Trailhead from Speedway/Campbell Intersection: 30 miles via Interstate 10; 23.6 miles via Old Spanish Trail

Directions to Trailhead from Speedway/Campbell Intersection: Via I-10: From the intersection of Speedway Boulevard and Campbell Avenue follow Campbell south toward I-10. Campbell turns left before the bridge that goes over 22nd Street. Do not continue on Campbell. Go straight ahead on what is now Kino Parkway to the junction of I-10. Follow I-10 to Exit 279. Turn left over I-10 toward Vail. Follow Colossal Cave Road for 3 miles to the intersection with Camino Loma Alta. Turn left on Camino Loma Alta. Follow Camino Loma Alta 5.5 miles to the Loma Alta Trailhead parking area. Via Old Spanish Trail: Follow Speedway east to the intersection of Camino Seco. Turn right on Camino Seco to the intersection of Old Spanish Trail. Turn left on Old Spanish Trail. Follow Old Spanish Trail to the intersection of Camino Loma Alta. Turn left on Camino Loma Alta for 2.2 miles to the Loma Alta Trailhead parking area.

Fees: Entrance to Saguaro National Park is $10 for any privately owned vehicle or motorcycle and $5 for any individual on foot or bicycle. Entry is valid for seven days. Several passes are also available: Saguaro National Park Annual Pass, $25, is valid for one year from the date of purchase;

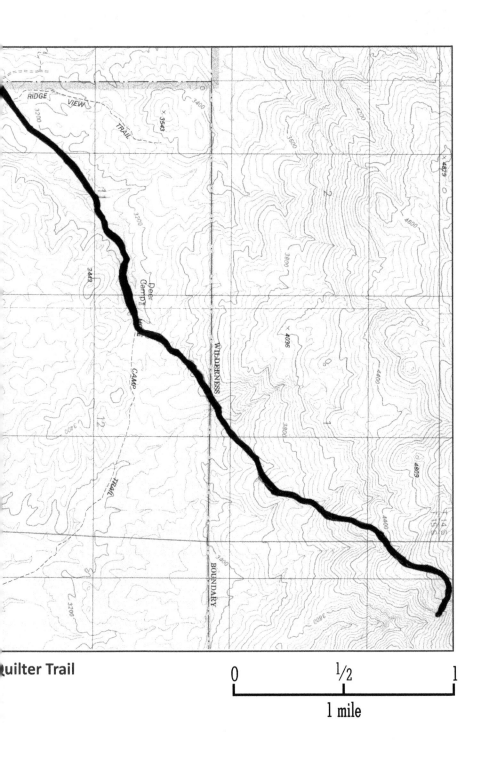

0   1/2   1

1 mile

Hiker climbing steps on the Quilter Trail.

America the Beautiful Annual Pass, $80; America the Beautiful, Senior Pass, $10, is a lifetime pass to National Park and Recreation Areas for US citizens age 62 and over; and the Access Pass, a lifetime pass for US citizens or permanent residents with permanent disabilities. Passes may be purchased at the Saguaro National Park Visitor Centers.

■ ■ ■

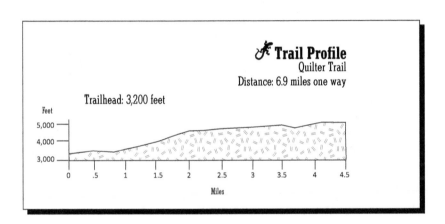

Trail Profile
Quilter Trail
Distance: 6.9 miles one way

John "Jake" Quilter helped build a new trail in the Rincon Mountains that is part of the Arizona Trail. He moved rocks to make steps to help hikers climb steep sections of the trail, lined rocks along the level sections to keep hikers from wandering off the trail, and trimmed tree branches that stretched across the trail. On April 26, 2011, as the trail crew climbed to their work site, Quilter ran ahead as he often did. When the rest of the crew reached the site, they found Quilter lying motioness on the trail. Tests would later show he died of heart failure. The Quilter Trail is named in his honor.

To reach the Quilter Trail, you must first walk 2.3 miles on the Hope Camp Trail, which begins on a gravel road through the gate of the Loma Alta Trailhead parking area. On your left are views of the high ridge that the Quilter Trail will partially climb. The road passes through a basin filled with mesquite trees before reaching the turnoff to the Quilter Trail. Just before the turnoff, look on the left for a large windmill and two large water tanks. This is Deer Camp, a "line camp" that was used during roundups when this area was a functioning ranch.

Watch carefully on the left for the turnoff of the Quilter Trail. The Quilter Trail remains level for a quarter mile and then begins to climb gradually towards the ridge. Most of the lower part of the trail goes through a saguaro forest. This is one of the most remarkable stands of saguaro in this area. There are many exceptionally large saguaro that are hundreds of years old. After crossing a large wash, the trail turns to the left and climbs steeply. The rock steps make this portion of the trail easier to climb.

About three-quarters of the way up the trail and on the left is an unusual saguaro. It's slightly below the trail and easy to miss. Instead of having arms that are spaced on the trunk of the saguaro, the arms are all sprouting out from the top of the plant. There are at least thirty-six arms, making the saguaro look like a large fan.

As you gain elevation the trail becomes more difficult. Compensating for the difficulty are the splendid views of the surrounding area. It takes an exceptionally strong hiker to reach the intersection with the Manning Camp Trail and return in one day. The first 4.6 miles will introduce you to the challenges of the Quilter Trail. Come back at the break of dawn another day to conquer the entire trail.

THE
SANTA CATALINA
MOUNTAINS

In A.D. 900 Hohokam women ground mesquite beans in summer camps high in the canyons of the Santa Catalina Mountains while their men hunted. Bedrock mortars and petroglyphs remain as evidence of their time in the mountains.

The Hohokam were gone and the Tohono O'odham Indians were living in the Tucson basin by the time Jesuit priest Father Kino established his mission at San Xavier del Bac in the late 1600s. Kino referred to the mountains to the north and east as the Santa Catarina Mountains, possibly in honor of Saint Catherine's Day. In time this changed to the Santa Catalina Mountains ... the Catalinas.

By the early 1800s, Apache Indians hunted and camped in the Catalinas and occasionally raided the settlements and the mission near Tucson. To protect their missions and route to California, the Spaniards built a fort on the site of what is today downtown Tucson. Apaches attacked the fort unsuccessfully and the Spaniards survived, until the Mexican War of Independence shifted ownership of Tucson to Mexico in 1821.

By 1854, when the United States government secured possession with the Gadsden Purchase, Anglos with the gleam of gold in their eyes began to move into Tucson. They built trails into the Catalinas, looking for gold, then silver and copper.

Others were interested in the Catalinas. Sara Plummer Lemmon and her husband came to the Catalinas in 1880. Botanists on their honeymoon, they rode horseback up from Oracle, guided by rancher E. O. Stratton. On the highest peak, the three carved their initials on a large pine and christened the peak Mount Lemmon, in honor of Sara. The name stuck and today the 9,157-foot-high point of the Santa Catalinas is still called Mount Lemmon.

By 1891 there were those who thought these mountains should be protected and Congress authorized the president to withdraw certain lands from the public domain. In 1902 the Catalina Forest Preserve was created. A conservationist president, Theodore Roosevelt, organized the National Forest Service in 1905, and by 1908 the Coronado National Forest was created.

More trails were built into the high country. Tucsonans camped there in the summer. Some leased land and built cabins. Much discussion was devoted to building a road up the mountain. By 1920 a rough road had been carved up to the top from Oracle, but Tucsonans wanted a "short road" from their side of the mountain.

After much maneuvering by the then editor/publisher of the *Tucson Citizen*, Frank Hitchcock, Secretary of Agriculture Henry A. Wallace approved a twenty-five-mile, two-lane, surfaced road up to the village of Summerhaven. The federal government would foot the bill, and the road would be built by prisoners. Construction began in 1933 and inched up the mountain. It was not completed until 1951. The road was named in honor of the man who got it all going, but who did not live to see it completed. The road, now called the Catalina Highway, was originally named in honor of the man who got it all going, but who did not live to see it completed

To protect the mountains from further development, in 1978 the Pusch Ridge Wilderness Area was created under the Endangered American Wilderness Act. In all, 56,933 acres, encompassing nearly the entire front range, are now closed to future development and all motorized vehicles. The only way to get to the heart of this spectacular area is on foot or horseback.

In the summer of 2003, a massive human-caused forest fire called the Aspen Fire struck the Santa Catalina Mountains, destroying more than 85,000 acres. The fire swept through the mountaintop town of Summerhaven, wiping out all of the businesses in town, except the post office and pie shop, and nearly 330 homes. Three trails in this section were badly damaged by the fire—Romero Canyon Trail, Gordon Hirabayashi Recreation Site to Sabino Canyon Trail, and the Box Camp Trail. Although the trails have now been reopened, there is still evidence of the fire.

Agua Caliente Hill Trail

General Description: An up-and-down trail through thick stands of saguaro cactus that provides incredible views of Tucson and surrounding mountain ranges

Difficulty: Difficult with areas of steep climbing

Best Time of Year to Hike: Winter, early spring, late fall

Length: 9.0 miles round-trip

Miles to Trailhead from Speedway/Campbell Intersection: 13 miles

Directions to Trailhead from Speedway/Campbell Intersection: Go east on Speedway to Houghton Road. Turn left on Houghton Road. Turn right at Fort Lowell. Fort Lowell becomes Camino Anchu. Turn left on Camino Remuda and follow it to the end. Camino Remuda veers left just before a house driveway. A large trailhead parking area is on the right.

■　■　■

Agua Caliente means "hot water" in Spanish. Agua Caliente Hill, Agua Caliente Wash, and Agua Caliente Springs are all named for the hot springs located in the area. By the early 1870s maps showing the location of the United States Army post at Camp Lowell also noted Agua Caliente Springs. In 1873 Peter Bain filed the first formal claim to the land surrounding the springs with the intent of grazing large herds of cattle. Two years later Bain sold his ranch to James Fuller.

In his article, "Agua Caliente," in the Winter 2002 *Journal of Arizona History*, author James Ayres reports that Fuller, in addition to running a large herd of cattle, "planted nearly 3,000 orange, date, pomegranate, quince, and fig trees." Fuller hired Tucson metallurgist and assayer W. T. Rickard to make a chemical analysis of the water from the springs. Rickard reported that the water possessed tonic qualities of a highest order. Fuller advertised his Agua Caliente Ranch as "a useful place of resort for sick people, or those who seek temporary recreation away from the heat and business of the city." Hikers climbing the Agua Caliente Hill Trail will get an overview of the area that was once the Fuller Ranch.

My son Rod and I chose a warm January day to make our first climb on Agua Caliente Hill. There's a bit of an age difference between us, and I suspected I would lag behind. We stopped at the beginning to admire a giant saguaro that stands to the left of the trail. With eleven arms and a height of approximately thirty feet, the saguaro must be well over 200 years old.

The first section of the trail climbs steeply. The climb is made easier by the steps dug into the hillside with large wood blocks to stop erosion. As the trail nears a fence, horses are routed around several particularly steep steps. I decided to follow the horse trail. At the top of this first steep part, we get our first of many views, each better than the last. From our vantage point we see Elephant Head at the base of the Santa Rita Mountains, Baboquivari, and Kitt Peak. I make a mental note to bring binoculars the next time I do this hike.

We follow a fairly level ridge for a half mile, noting the changing vegetation. Along the trail there are large patches of my least favorite desert plant, a member of the agave family known locally as "shindaggers." It's the hiker's nemesis! We also note large numbers of saguaro of all sizes growing on the south side of the hills, with virtually none growing on the northern slopes. The southern slopes get more sunshine, thus encouraging growth of the saguaros.

After climbing to another lookout point where we have views of the front range of the Santa Catalinas, we see a large earthen dam far below. At first glance we think this will be an easy jaunt down to what the map calls Cat Track Tank, but we learn that we will go down into and climb out of several ravines and dry washes before reaching the tank. It is evident that cattle gather around Cat Track Tank.

Past the tank we make yet another steep climb to yet another ridge high above the cattle tank. Here a sign indicates that it is 3 miles back

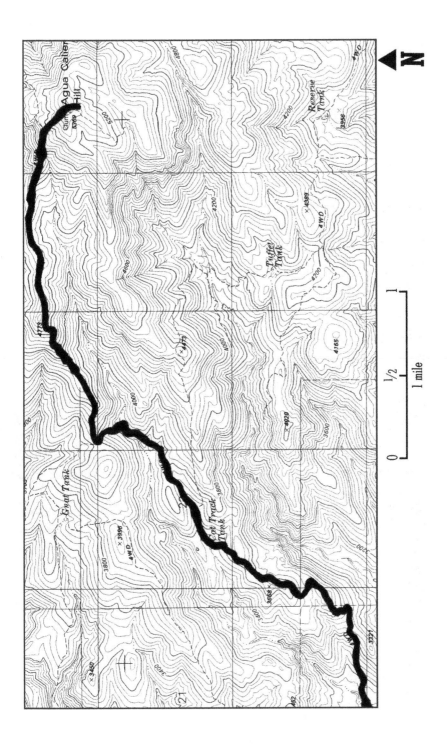

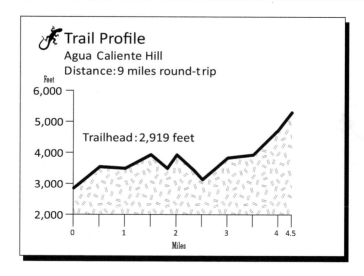

Trail Profile
Agua Caliente Hill
Distance: 9 miles round-trip

to the trailhead. It seemed much longer than that! In 1.5 miles we would be standing on the summit of Agua Caliente Hill.

Far ahead we see the top of a hill that we think is Agua Caliente Hill. The trail now becomes an old Forest Service road and is easy to walk. We are high above the saguaro now. We are headed up, straight, we think, to the base of Agua Caliente Hill. I anticipate the spectacular views we will get from the summit. A few more steps and we realize that the trail is not headed directly to the top of the hill; rather, it appears to be bearing to the right. My son says, "I hope this isn't 'False Hope Hill.'" False Hope Hill it became as the trail curved around the base of the hill and continued on toward what we now realized was the real Agua Caliente Hill.

A discussion ensued. It was getting late, and we needed to head back down. Rod, suggesting that since he was faster than I, would jog on to check out the summit ahead while I bushwhacked to the top of what we now knew was False Hope Hill to see if there was a marker on top.

I started climbing, trying to avoid the shindaggers. I soon discovered that False Hope Hill deserved its name. It was not one, but two small hills separated by a steep cliff. To get to the actual summit, where I thought the marker would be located, I had to go partway back down the hill and climb up again. After searching in vain for a United States Geological Survey (USGS) marker, I found a comfortable rock to sit on and enjoy the views.

En route to Agua Caliente Hill.

I watched as my son in his red jacket made it to the summit. I met him at the base of False Hope Hill. He described the trail to the summit as extremely difficult, with loose rocks. "Take a hiking stick when you climb it," he warned. He found two USGS markers on the summit, dated 1947. He did report that the views were the best so far. Next time I'll start earlier in the day so I can make it to the top. About my lagging behind? Maybe a little!

Bug Spring Trail

General Description: A hike with spectacular views of surrounding mountains

Difficulty: Difficult with some areas of steep climbing or descent

Best Time of Year to Hike: Spring, fall, winter

Length: 4.6 miles one way

Miles to Trailhead from Speedway/Campbell Intersection: 26 miles

Directions to Trailhead from Speedway/Campbell Intersection: These directions are for hiking from the Green Mountain/Bug Spring Trailhead at Milepost 11 and require two vehicles. Go east on Speedway to the intersection of Wilmot, turn left on Wilmot. Wilmot becomes Tanque Verde Road at the Pima intersection. Follow Tanque Verde Road to the Catalina Highway. Turn left on Catalina Highway to the Bug Springs Trailhead, which is just past Milepost 7 and on the right. Leave one vehicle here and continue up the Catalina Highway to just past Milepost 11 to the Green Mountain/Bug Spring Trailhead, which is on your right. The Bug Spring Trail begins on the lower corner of the trailhead where a large sign depicts the trail.

■　■　■

Hike the Bug Spring Trail from the Bug Spring Trailhead just past Milepost 7 on the Catalina Highway and you'll gain 1,400 feet. Hike it from the Green Mountain/Bug Spring Trailhead at Milepost 11 and you'll gain 600 feet. It took a nanosecond for me to figure out where I wanted to start!

I enticed three fellow hikers to join me on a beautiful fall morning. We dropped one car off at the Bug Spring Trailhead and all climbed into my car to continue up to the Green Mountain/Bug Spring Trailhead. We studied the trailhead sign at the lower corner of the parking area and learned that we were headed to Lower Bug Spring. Upper Bug Spring is located near the beginning of the Green Mountain Trail.

We started up the trail. Yes, I said "Up!" Even though we were 1,000 feet above our final destination, we had to go up before we could start down. Wide steps made of boards made it easier to climb the steep hill. In places the trail leveled out, only to start up again with more steps.

Near the top of the first ridge we started down into the canyon on the south side of the ridge. In the canyon we hiked under Chihuahua pine, alligator juniper, and silverleaf oak. We crossed the creek bed several times. Although there was no water in the creek, there would likely be water during the winter months and in early spring. The hike was shady and cool.

As the canyon opened up, we climbed about an eighth of a mile to the top of the ridge. The views opened up and we were awestruck. We could see the outline of the mountain ranges near Tucson—the Rincons, Santa Ritas, Tortillas, Tucson Mountains—and most of the city.

The trail continued along the ridge through an area of oddly shaped rock formations called hoodoos. A hoodoo is a tall spire of rock ranging in height from that of an average human to heights exceeding a ten-

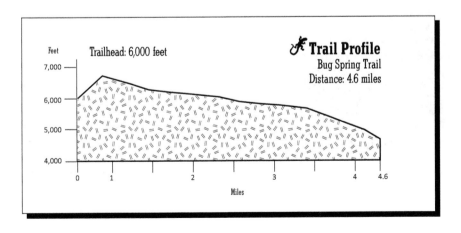

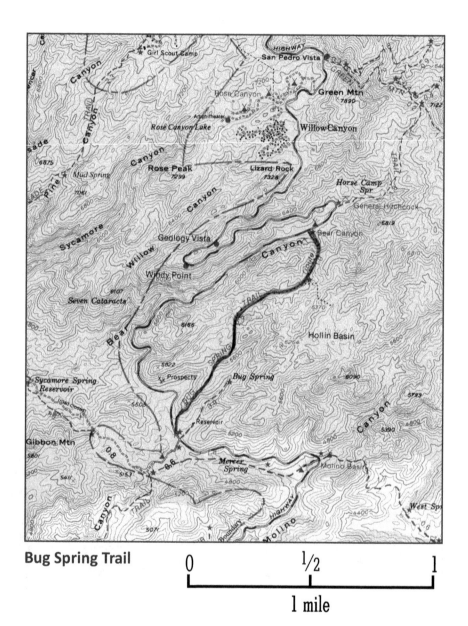

Bug Spring Trail

0   1/2   1

1 mile

Hikers pausing beside hoodoo formations.

story building. Hoodoos are mainly found in the desert in dry, hot areas. Hikers enjoy giving names to some of the formations.

We started down through an area damaged by the Aspen Fire in 2003. As we neared the end of the trail, we could see some buildings near lower Bug Spring. I had hoped to explore the spring after we completed the hike, but access to the road leading to the spring is prohibited.

Lower Bug Spring was used from 1939 until 1967 to supply water to the prison camp directly across the Catalina Highway, now known as the Gordon Hirabayashi Recreation Site, that housed Japanese-Americans during World War II. After the war, inmates convicted of breaking federal immigration or tax laws or who were conscientious objectors were sent to the camp. The prisoners built the General Hitchcock Highway up Mount Lemmon. The roadway was completed in 1961 and is now called the Catalina Highway

When you reach the bottom of the hill, turn right to the Bug Springs Trailhead. The trail to the left leads across the road to the Hirabayashi Recreation Site. Climb into the waiting vehicle and drive up to the Green Mountain/Bug Spring Trailhead to retrieve your other vehicle.

Mount Lemmon to Catalina State Park

General Description: A long, spectacular hike from Mount Lemmon to Catalina State Park via the Mount Lemmon and Romero Canyon Trails

Difficulty: Extremely difficult, sections of steep, rocky descent

Best Time of Year to Hike: Spring, fall

Length: 13.1 miles one way

Miles to Trailhead from Speedway/Campbell Intersection: 42 miles

Directions to Trailhead from Speedway/Campbell Intersection: Go east on Speedway to the intersection of Wilmot. Turn left on Wilmot. Wilmot becomes Tanque Verde Road. Continue on Tanque Verde Road 4.2 miles to the Catalina Highway. Turn left on Catalina Highway. Drive 32.6 miles up the Catalina Highway past the Iron Door Restaurant until the highway ends at the entrance to the University of Arizona Observatory. The section of road past the Iron Door Restaurant is closed from December 15 to March 1. You will need to arrange transportation to Mount Lemmon and at Catalina State Park.

■ ■ ■

The hike from Mount Lemmon to Catalina State Park is one of the most difficult hikes in the mountains surrounding Tucson. When my friend Jim Bowen said he'd been wanting to hike from Mount Lemmon through Romero Canyon to Catalina State Park for years, I said, "Let's do it!"

Jim made all the arrangements. He recruited his hiking friends and neighbors, Carleen Jenko and Lisa Foster, to join us. Lisa brought her friend Jon Bayers, recently graduated from law school, to join us on the trek. Jim's friends, Joe and Winnie Doerfer, volunteered to drive us up. They left their neighborhood at 6:00 A.M. and picked me up at 6:15 A.M. at the Safeway parking lot at Swan and Campbell. Jim's wife, Pat, planned to meet us in Catalina State Park at the Romero Canyon Trailhead around 4:00 P.M. The hike, according to a friend of Jim's who had hiked this route, would take about seven hours.

The drive up to Mount Lemmon was pleasant. We arrived at the trailhead for the Mount Lemmon Trail where the elevation was 9,157 feet and there was frost on the ground. It was late October and the aspen had turned golden. We pulled on our jackets and headed down the trail. The time was 8:00 A.M. We would lose 6,507 feet of elevation by the time we reached the end of our hike!

The trail starts under tall pines and after a mile of steep downhill enters the area called the Wilderness of Rocks. On rest breaks we gave names to the rock formations. "Look, there's Snoopy!" Lisa said, pointing to the rim high above us. Carleen countered with "Look at the Sleeping Clown!"

As the sun rose higher, we shed our jackets. Occasional uphill portions of the trail gave our legs relief from the constant downhill. We thought we were alone on the trail until we heard voices approaching. Soon a group of hikers from British Columbia, Canada, caught up with us. They were doing a loop hike and turned left on the Wilderness of Rocks trail.

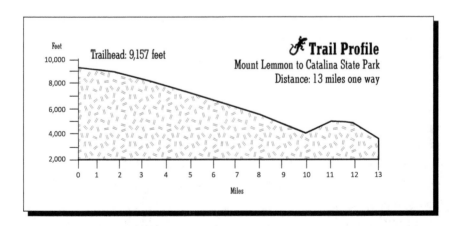

Looking down the Mount Lemmon Trail to Catalina State Park.

We continued past the Wilderness of Rocks trail turnoff and reached the intersection of the Romero Canyon Trail about 1:00 P.M. The elevation at the Romero Canyon Trailhead was 6,080 feet. We had started at 9,157 feet. When we reached the trailhead at Catalina State Park we would be at 2,650 feet. Do the math!

Surely we would make it to Catalina State Park before dark! We had 7.2 miles to go, all downhill except for a short climb past Romero Pools. The views were still spectacular. By now we could see the outline of Picacho Peak to the North.

The trail became more difficult. There were many areas of steep, rocky declines where we had to walk slowly. Still, we made progress. By 4:00 P.M., as we paused for a brief rest, Carleen said, "Look, there's Wal-Mart!" From then on we joked about going to WalMart. Jim tried to call Pat, who by now was waiting at the trailhead, to tell her we were running "a bit" late but the phone read "No Service."

A few miles later someone commented about being on the Romeo Trail. "It's not Romeo," I said quickly. "It is Romero Trail named after

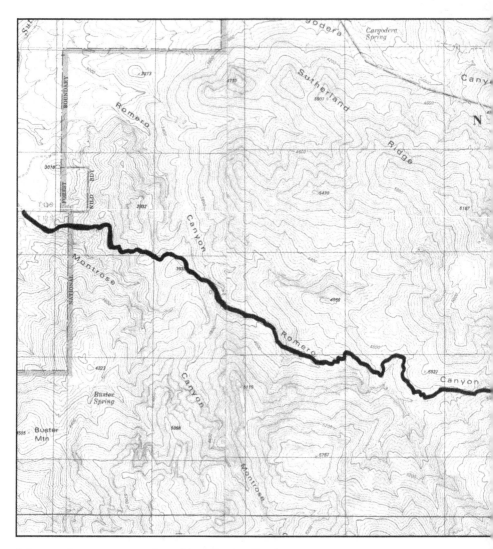

Mount Lemmon to Catalina State Park

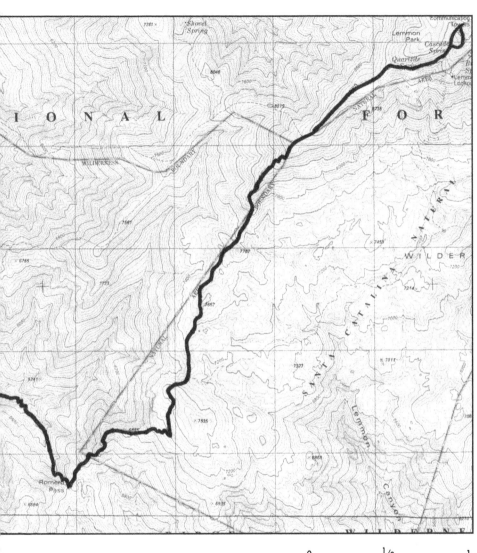

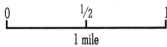

Fabian Romero, who established Rancho Romero in this area in 1889. The ranch covered 4,800 acres." I could have elaborated more, but no one seemed interested. My fellow hikers were more concerned about the sun sinking in the west.

By the time we reached Romero Pools it was nearly dark. The sun had disappeared from the sides of the mountains. A lone star shone in the sky. Jim put on his headlamp. His was the only light in the group. We hiked slowly as the sky filled with stars. The moon? No sign of it.

We kept thinking the trail would smooth out. It didn't. We developed a strategy. Jim would go over the rough parts of the trail first, then shine his light back for the rest of us to come down. It took seemingly forever. Jim finally reached Pat on his cell phone. He told her we were running a bit late and that it would be at least 9:00 P.M. before we reached the trailhead.

At 9:15 P.M. we saw the trailhead sign. We walked quickly toward the parking lot where Pat waved her flashlight. We made it! No sprained ankles! No broken bones! Just very tired legs. Would we do it again? Of course!

Blackett's Ridge Trail

General Description: A short hike on a ridge between Sabino and Bear Canyons, with spectacular views of Tucson and the canyons

Difficulty: Moderate, steep for the first mile

Best Time of Year to Hike: Early spring, late fall, winter

Length: 4.6 miles round-trip

Miles to Trailhead from Speedway/Campbell Intersection: 11.1 miles

Directions to Trailhead from Speedway/Campbell Intersection: Go east on Speedway 5 miles to Wilmot Road. Turn left. Wilmot becomes Tanque Verde at the Pima intersection. Continue on Tanque Verde to Sabino Canyon Road. Turn left and follow the signs to the Sabino Canyon Visitor Center parking lot. The trailhead can be reached by tram or by walking 0.8 of a mile across the desert and on the road (see text below).

Fees: The fee to park in Sabino Canyon is $5 per day. The America the Beautiful cards, which are $80 for an Annual Pass, $10 for a lifetime Senior Pass, and free of charge for an Access Pass available to permanently disabled US citizens, are also accepted as is the Coronado Recreation Pass, which is $5 for a daily pass, $10 for a weekly pass, and $20 for an annual pass. Both cards are available for purchase at the Sabino Canyon Visitor Center. Put the card on the dashboard of your vehicle.

■ ■ ■

Blackett's Ridge is one of the best little hikes in the Tucson area. This ridge was named by Don Everett, a teacher at the Southern Arizona

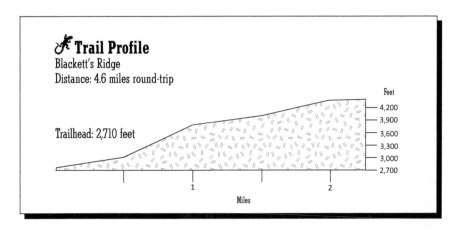

🦎 **Trail Profile**

Blackett's Ridge

Distance: 4.6 miles round-trip

Trailhead: 2,710 feet

Feet
- 4,200
- 3,900
- 3,600
- 3,300
- 3,000
- 2,700

Miles

School for Boys, after one of his students. In 1937 Everett made the first ascent of the ridge on horseback, accompanied by Hill Blackett, Jr., a student from Winnetka, Illinois. From that day, the ridge has been called Blackett's Ridge.

You can reach the trailhead by riding the Bear Canyon Tram, or, if you prefer, by walking on the wide path that crosses the desert from the east end of the Sabino Canyon parking lot. The trail starts between two brick pillars. When you reach the paved road, continue walking to the right, passing to the right of the rest rooms, across the bridge, and again to the right where a small sign on your left indicates several trails including the Blackett's Ridge Trail. If you are riding the tram, tell the driver that you want off at Stop 2, where you'll walk across the bridge and turn right to the trailhead. (To return by tram, you must be at the Stop 2 sign for pickup.)

After 100 yards, there is a signed trail intersection. Turn left at the intersection, following the Phoneline Trail to the cutoff for the Blackett's Ridge Trail. This trail follows the route of an old phone line to Mount Lemmon and is popular with joggers, who like to run up the trail and down the road, and with hikers, who ride the tram up Sabino Canyon and hike down the trail.

There is a very gradual elevation gain on smooth trail, through the typical vegetation of this elevation. After 0.4 of a mile you come to a signed turnoff to the right that leads to Blackett's Ridge. It takes about twenty minutes of leisurely hiking to reach this turnoff.

Straight ahead and high above is Blackett's Ridge. The Phoneline Trail continues up the canyon, and the trail to Blackett's Ridge begins to switchback up the ridge. After about a quarter of a mile, Sabino Canyon is visible, and you can see the tram. If the wind is right, you can hear the narration of the tram guide. Sabino Creek is visible, as is a small dam. In 1910 and again in the 1930s, private companies and government agencies made serious proposals to dam part of Sabino Canyon for use as Tucson's water and electric supply. Had any of these projects materialized, the views from Blackett's Ridge would be quite different!

The switchbacks become very steep and shorter as you come to the top of the front part of the trail. You level off briefly and wind around to the south side of the ridge. The Santa Ritas are now directly in front of you. In winter, which is the best time to do this hike, Mount

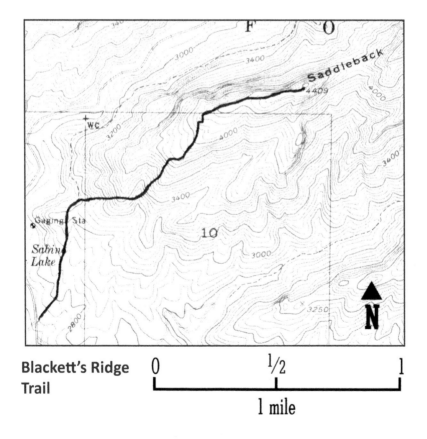

Blackett's Ridge Trail

0   ½   1

1 mile

Wrightson is usually snow covered, as are the Rincon Mountains to the east. As the trail continues, the switchbacks get even steeper, and soon the road leading to Bear Canyon is visible. A tram runs hourly to the popular Seven Falls Trailhead.

You quickly come to the first of several good lookout points. It is as if you were driving through the Rocky Mountains and come to signs saying, "Scenic Pullout." There are several such "pullouts" along the first part of this trail that are good places from which to sit and observe the valley below. By the way, there are no official pullouts—you will find your own.

As you recover from the steep climb, survey the sights. The greens of the Ventana Canyon golf course are in sharp contrast to the desert. By now, the parking lot of Sabino Canyon looks like a small asphalt square.

The trail continues gaining elevation and the "pullouts" get better and better. Soon you have an excellent view up Sabino Canyon and into the heart of the Catalinas. You then come to a long, smooth saddle, and you know you are definitely on a narrow ridge between two canyons. On the right are the Rincons and Santa Ritas, and on the left are the Catalinas and Sabino Canyon.

As you cross the saddle, the trail again becomes rocky and climbs toward what looks like the high point of the ridge. Topped by a big pile of rocks, this high point is the first of three false summits. The trail is distinct and climbs gradually, going to the left of what appeared to be the high point.

As the trail ascends toward a second apparent summit, it bears slightly to the right and becomes quite steep. The area on the right was burned several years ago, and many of the saguaros show evidence of the fire. They are black around the bottom but still green at the top. They appear to be alive, but only time will tell if they will ultimately survive.

Straight ahead is a magnificent view of Thimble Peak; at 5,323 feet, it is the highest point in Sabino Canyon. The views from up here are great, but you do realize that the actual summit of Blackett's Ridge is still a few hundred yards ahead.

The trail ends abruptly. Climbing expertise is required for any further exploration of the ridge. Extreme caution must be exercised in this area. The cliffs to the left, called the Acropolis Cliffs by the tram drivers, drop 400 feet into Sabino Canyon. A misstep could be tragic.

However dangerous the summit of Blackett's Ridge, it does provide literally breathtaking views into Sabino Canyon. The Phoneline Trail has become a narrow ribbon. The now tiny-looking trams traverse the road, their drivers introducing tourists to the diversity of Sabino Canyon. As you sit quietly, you can hear the rush of water in Sabino Creek, occasionally mingled with the voices of people. Birds dive down the cliffs, and occasionally deer can be spotted as they head to the water below. The four mountain ranges surrounding Tucson make an unforgettable panorama.

It takes about an hour to return to the parking lot. The Blackett's Ridge hike is a good morning's workout, one that you will return to many times.

Blackett's Ridge.

Esperero Trail

General Description: A long hike over rugged terrain, with dramatic views of the Tucson Valley

Difficulty: Extremely difficult

Best Time of Year to Hike: Early spring, late fall

Length: 16.8 miles round-trip

Miles to Trailhead from Speedway/Campbell Intersection: 11.1 miles to the Sabino Canyon parking lot

Directions to Trailhead from Speedway/Campbell Intersection: Go east on Speedway 5 miles to Wilmot Road. Turn left. Wilmot becomes Tanque Verde at the Pima intersection. Continue on Tanque Verde to Sabino Canyon Road. Turn left and follow the signs to the Sabino Canyon Visitor Center parking lot. It is 0.7 of a mile up the Sabino Canyon Road to the trailhead.

Fees: The fee to park in Sabino Canyon is $5 per day. The America the Beautiful cards, which are $80 for an Annual Pass, $10 for a lifetime Senior Pass, and free of charge for an Access Pass available to permanently disabled US citizens, are also accepted as is the Coronado Recreation Pass, which is $5 for a daily pass, $10 for a weekly pass, and $20 for an annual pass. Both cards are available for purchase at the Sabino Canyon Visitor Center. Put the card on the dashboard of your vehicle.

■　■　■

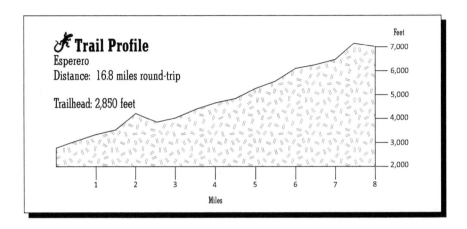

🦎 Trail Profile
Esperero
Distance: 16.8 miles round-trip

Trailhead: 2,850 feet

Esperero Trail begins in Sabino Canyon and climbs 8.4 miles to a twenty-five-foot opening in the crest of a ridge known as the Window. Elevation at the trailhead is 2,850 feet—at the end you'll be at 7,000 feet and be able to see most of Tucson. The trail, originally known as the Dixie Saddle Trail, was constructed in 1924 by Forest Service workers as a trail for use by horseback riders and was described in an early newspaper account as a trail on which "natural wonders meet the gaze at every turn." The reason the name was changed to *Esperero*, Spanish for "hopeful," is unknown.

Park in the visitor lot at Sabino Canyon and begin walking up the asphalt road into the canyon. At 0.7 of a mile you will see a sign on the left indicating the Cactus Picnic Area. A few yards past the sign and on the left, another sign indicates Esperero Trail.

The first section of the trail is heavily used because it is near the Cactus Picnic Area and several side trails may confuse you. The correct route is level for about 100 yards and then uphill and to the right. The sign at this junction is frequently vandalized and may be missing when you attempt this hike. At the top of the first hill you reach a signed trail intersection. To the right is a trail that drops into Sabino Canyon. Here, you want to turn left. As you look backward, you realize that you have already gained considerable elevation. From this spot you can see the observatory on Kitt Peak and much of the Tucson Valley.

Beyond the intersection, the trail levels and then drops into Rattlesnake Canyon. Rattlesnakes deter some people from hiking in the

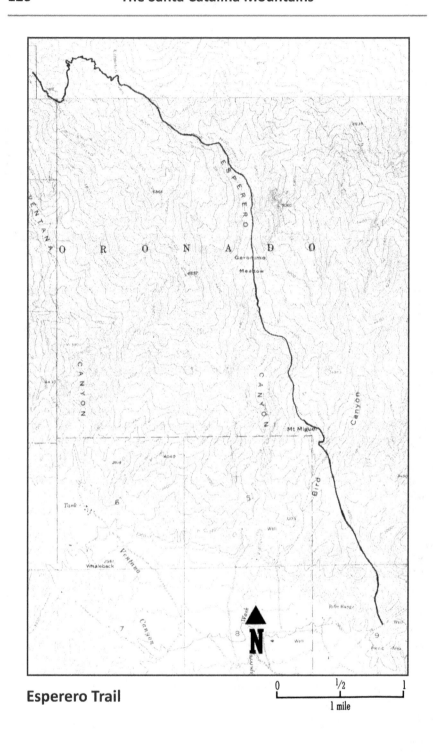

Esperero Trail

0   ½   1

1 mile

Catalinas. True, Arizona does have more rattlers than any other state in the Union, but, in twenty years of hiking these mountains, I have only seen two. If you see or hear a rattler, stay away from it, and be familiar with proper treatment procedures, which are given in the front of this guide.

The next part of the trail can be confusing. Where there is danger of getting off the trail, low barriers of sticks and stones block the way. Also, cairns mark the trail in critical spots. After about a mile of strenuous climbing, you level off and then make a sharp descent into Bird Canyon. Here the trail has been rerouted to avoid a short section of private land. As you will note, folks are building homes quite close to the forest boundary.

The vegetation along the trail thus far is typical of the 3,000-foot to 4,000-foot elevation range in the Sonoran Desert—saguaro, barrel, prickly pear, and cholla cacti, ocotillos, mesquite, and palo verde trees, and assorted shrubs, including creosote bush and brittlebush. You may spot deer, javelina, or coyote. Small lizards scatter as you hike. If you are interested in identifying those lizards, the Sabino Canyon Visitor Center in Sabino Canyon has an information sheet that identifies twelve species of lizards. The problem is getting them to hold still long enough for you to identify them!

The trail climbs out of Bird Canyon and then drops into Esperero Canyon. A series of steep step-ups makes this one of the more difficult sections of Esperero, as it hugs the side of the drainage for nearly a mile. It is also one of the prettiest sections, with many large saguaros clinging miraculously to what appears to be barren rock.

Once you come out of the drainage, the real hike begins. It is here that shindaggers make their appearance. Apparently placed here by the "great protector of the Catalinas," this wicked plant has sharp daggers at shin level and attacks anyone who wanders too far off the trail.

This quarter-mile section of the trail between the drainage and the ridge top has been nicknamed "cardiac gap" by local hikers. Don't let the nickname deter you—it's not that bad. A series of switchbacks get you to the top of the ridge. Go slowly and enjoy the view as the city below spreads out across the valley. The flashing tower lights of Tucson Electric Power's substation are easy to spot. Persist, and before you realize it, you are on top of cardiac gap. It takes the average hiker two and

Bridal Veil Falls on the Esperero Trail.

one-half to three hours to reach this point, approximately three miles.

The ridge is an excellent lunch spot. Turn your back to the city, and the magnificent Catalinas seem to go on forever. Cathedral Rock is the dominant formation of this part of the range. Below, providing there has been enough rainfall, there is a large waterfall where Esperero Canyon empties into the basin. From this point it takes about two hours to return to the Sabino Canyon parking lot. This is a good turnaround point for your first attempt at Esperero Trail.

If you choose to continue, Esperero has a lot more to offer. The trail drops down on the north side of the ridge slightly, climbs steadily for about a quarter of a mile, and then levels out and circles the basin. Although you are no longer climbing as steeply as before, this section of the trail is still difficult. It is rocky and there are steep step-ups. Since very few people traverse this section, it is usually overgrown and can be tricky to negotiate. Several varieties of oak, juniper, piñon pine, and manzanita grow at this elevation, approximately 5,000 feet. The trail at this point is rugged and overgrown. Not many people make it this far. Congratulate yourself, eat a high-energy bar, and plunge ahead!

Less than a mile from the ridge, the trail passes a large outcropping of rocks on the left and enters Geronimo Meadow. Geronimo Meadow is not a meadow by most definitions. The "meadow" is a level area filled with manzanita and a few pine. There is a good camping spot, complete with a large fire ring and a log to sit on.

Beyond the meadow the trail drops sharply into Esperero Canyon. A creek flows sporadically, mostly in early spring. The trail follows the creek, crisscrossing it several times. If you think you're off the trail, look for cairns. A heavy stand of tall oak trees shades the trail, and this part of the hike is quite pleasant.

One mile upstream, you come to Mormon Spring. A sign indicates a concrete tank off to the right that, in all except the driest season, is filled with water. There are also several pools above the spring that nearly always have water. Don't drink from either source unless you have a way to purify the water.

Beyond Mormon Spring, it's another half mile to Bridal Veil Falls. The trail is overgrown, difficult to follow, and very steep in places, but the waterfalls at the end make it all worthwhile. About 50 feet tall and surrounded by towering pines, it resembles a bride's veil when sufficient rainfall creates a spray. Even when there has been very little rain, there is usually a trickle, enough for a refreshing shower on a hot afternoon. By the time you reach the waterfall, you will have hiked 5.5 miles and gained 2,450 feet in elevation—a respectable day's hike.

Only very well-conditioned, experienced hikers should continue the final 2.9 miles to the Window. In winter the trail could be icy or covered with snow, and the short days may not allow time to return before dark. If you do continue on, expect some major climbing above Bridal Veil Falls and a final sharp descent before you stand in the Window at 7,000 feet. (A shorter route to the Window is via the Ventana Canyon Trail.) In its entirety, Esperero is one of the most difficult trails in the Catalinas. It is also, as you will see in your view from the Window, one of the most rewarding.

Ventana Canyon Trail

General Description: A challenging hike through one of the most beautiful canyons in the front range of the Catalinas

Difficulty: Difficult, some areas of steep climbing

Best Time of Year to Hike: Spring, fall

Length: 12.8 miles round-trip

Miles to Trailhead from Speedway/Campbell Intersection: 12.2 miles

Directions to Trailhead from Speedway/Campbell Intersection: Go east on Speedway 5 miles to Wilmot Road. Turn left. Wilmot becomes Tanque Verde at the Pima intersection. Continue on Tanque Verde to Sabino Canyon Road. Turn left on Sabino Canyon Road and go 3.7 miles to the intersection of Kolb Road. Continue straight ahead on Kolb Road for 3.4 miles past the entrance to Loew's Ventana Canyon Resort. Take the next right to the employee parking lot. A section in the back is reserved for hikers. The trail begins at the northwest corner of the parking lot.

■　■　■

As you look toward the Catalinas from the Grant-Campbell area, if the light is just right, you can see a tiny hole at the top of the mountain in about the middle of the range. That "tiny" hole is in a large rock fin at the crest of a ridge far above Ventana Canyon and is an oval opening approximately 15 feet high and 25 feet wide, known as the Window, or *Ventana* in Spanish. It is a challenging 6.4-mile climb up the Ventana Canyon Trail to the Window. Beginning at a 2,950-foot elevation, amid saguaro and mesquite, you eventually reach 7,000 feet,

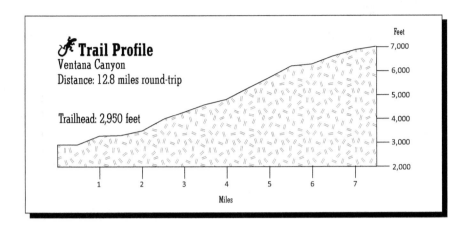

🦎 Trail Profile

Ventana Canyon

Distance: 12.8 miles round-trip

Trailhead: 2,950 feet

Feet
- 7,000
- 6,000
- 5,000
- 4,000
- 3,000
- 2,000

Miles: 1 2 3 4 5 6 7

where ponderosa pines tower above you. The nearly 13-mile round-trip hike will take most of the day.

Access to the Ventana Canyon Trail is on the property of the Ventana Canyon Resort until it reaches the National Forest boundary. Past the walk-through fence, the steep cliffs of Ventana Canyon rise spectacularly on each side. The trail follows the creek for about a mile. The creek is dry most of the year, but in late winter and spring it is usually running. After about a mile and a half, you begin to climb out of the bottom of the canyon, up a series of steep switchbacks. There are concrete slabs at intervals across this section of the trail that, although they prevent erosion, make walking more treacherous. This portion of the trail has splendid views of the city below and the Santa Rita Mountains south of Tucson. As you top the first set of switchbacks, you can see part of the golf course of the resort.

You top the hill and circle to the west before dropping down into an area known as Maiden Pools. This is a beautiful section of the canyon with a series of pools, a few large enough for swimming. It is easy to visualize how the area got its name—a beautiful maiden would look right at home here, sunbathing amid the pools and lush vegetation. Flowers and grasses grow in abundance. Large Mexican blue oaks provide shade, and there are many perfect picnic spots. This is a good turn-around point for a half-day hike, because it takes less than two hours to reach this point.

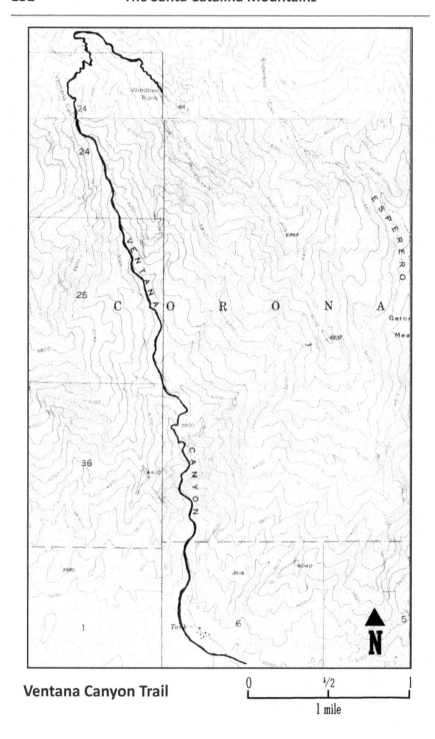

Ventana Canyon Trail

0   ½   1

1 mile

If you plan to continue to the Window, be aware that at Maiden Pools it is very easy to get off the trail, because there are many side trails that lead down to the pools. The trail to the Window stays above the pool area. If you take a side trail, be sure to come back up the same trail you went down and connect with the main trail.

Above Maiden Pools the trail is quite confusing for about a mile. It crosses the creek several times, and some parts are very brushy. Watch carefully for cairns that indicate direction.

About a mile past Maiden Pools, you come to a second pool area, smaller than Maiden Pools, but equally pretty. Several large Arizona sycamores, distinguished by the white sections of peeling bark, grow in this area. The canyon here is quite narrow and the pools are below the trail on the canyon floor.

Past the sycamores the climbing begins in earnest. There is a steep section where you gain elevation rapidly, first with a few switchbacks, then continuing nearly straight up. About halfway up this section is a large, smooth rock with two deep bedrock mortars, circular depressions caused by Indian women grinding mesquite beans or other legumes. This is evidence that at one time, nearly 1,000 years ago, Hohokam Indians camped and hunted in this canyon.

A few steps past the mortars look to the right and you will get your first view of the Window. From this vantage point, it looks impossible that you will actually be sitting in the Window in about two miles. The steep rock face with the still-tiny-looking opening appears formidable. You can easily see that a fall from the Window would be fatal.

Past the mortars rock, the trail goes through a pretty section. It passes a spring, where there are several small pools of water, and enters a section of ponderosa pine, an indication that you are nearing the highest elevations of the front range of the Catalinas. For a time, you are going directly away from the Window, heading west, and you may question whether you are on the correct trail. Then you make a sharp turn and head directly east toward the Window, switchbacking out of the canyon. About halfway up the switchbacks is a signed trail intersection. From here you can join the Finger Rock Trail and go 2.3 miles east to Mount Kimball. At this intersection, turn right for the final 1.2-mile climb to the Window.

Approach to the Window on the Ventana Canyon Trail.

Beyond the sign is a steep, rocky portion of the trail. It crosses the open side of the hill, and here it is very easy to lose your way. Watch carefully for cairns. You will want to rest often, and fortunately there are excellent views of the valley. As you come to the top of the switchbacks, you have a pleasant surprise. For about a half mile the trail crosses a saddle and is level. Your legs by this point really don't know how to walk on level ground. After about a quarter mile on the level area, there is a viewpoint to the left of the trail that provides dramatic views of the other side of the mountain. Biosphere II, the massive greenhouse that once housed sealed researchers, is now an environmental research station owned by the University of Arizona. Biosphere II is far off to the right. You can see several new housing developments and, forty miles north, the triangular outline of Picacho Peak.

The last quarter of a mile climbs steadily to the Window and is a killer, not because it is so terribly steep, but because your legs quickly adjusted to walking on level ground, and, after six miles of climbing, you're tired. When you reach the base of a large rock outcropping, you are almost there. Climb carefully over rocks along the base of the cliff and, suddenly, you are looking at the back of the Window.

I cannot emphasize enough the danger of climbing carelessly in the Window. Remember how it looked from the trail? It's at least 100 feet straight down. There is a safe, flat ledge for eating lunch and looking at the views. You can see the University of Arizona, the west side of Tucson, and the downtown area. The *A* on "A" Mountain is a tiny letter. Baboquivari Peak is visible and. on a very clear day, you can see the telescopes at the Kitt Peak Observatory.

After your hike, when you are stopped at the traffic light at Glenn and Campbell headed north, look to your right high up into the Catalinas. If the light is just right, you'll see a tiny opening. Now you know what's really there.

Pontatoc Ridge Trail

General Description: A short, fun hike to the top of a ridge in the front range of the Santa Catalinas

Difficulty: Moderate, short areas of steep climbing

Best Time of Year to Hike: Spring, fall, winter

Length: 5.2 miles round-trip

Miles to Trailhead from Speedway/Campbell Intersection: 8.4 miles

Directions to Trailhead from Speedway/Campbell Intersection: Go north on Campbell Avenue 6.2 miles to Skyline Drive. Turn right on Skyline Drive for 0.5 of a mile. At this point Skyline divides and turns left. Continue on Skyline for 0.7 of a mile to the intersection of Alvernon Way. Turn left on Alvernon Way, which dead-ends after 1 mile. The Richard "Dick" McGee Trailhead is on the left. Turn in carefully to avoid the wrong way spikes.

■ ■ ■

The Pontatoc Ridge Trail is named after the Pontotoc Mine. According to Lutie Wilson, who lives in the renovated cookshack of the mine, her husband Link's uncle, Miles Carpenter, located the mine in 1907. When he located the mine, a group of Indians lived around a nearby spring that had grapevines. The Indians called the area *pontotoc*, which is a Chickasaw Indian word meaning "hanging grapes."

Carpenter and two partners formed the Texas-Arizona Mining Company. Wilson says Carpenter mined three million dollars in copper, silver, and gold from the Pontotoc Mine. Carpenter became promi-

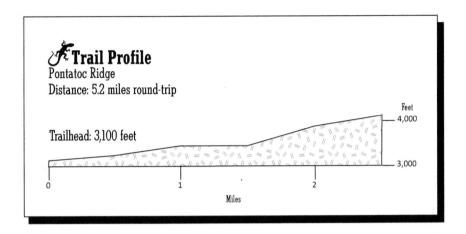

Trail Profile
Pontatoc Ridge
Distance: 5.2 miles round-trip

Trailhead: 3,100 feet

nent in mining circles until his death in 1942. Following his death, his widow, Dora, sold the Pontotoc Mine to Link and Lutie Wilson. The shafts are fenced, but Lutie still uses water from the mine to water her citrus trees.

On early maps of Tucson, the mine is spelled "Pontotoc," the same as two Chickasaw Indian towns in Mississippi and Oklahoma. By the early 1950s, the spelling had changed to "Pontatoc." This spelling error entered officialdom when the area around the mine was made into the Coronado Foothills Estates in 1961.

For the first few yards the Pontatoc Trail is part of the Finger Rock Trail. At the top of the first climb, a sign indicates that the Pontatoc Trail cuts off to the right. This trail was rerouted to skirt new development in the area.

As you begin, look to the northeast. A stark triangular ridge, with what appears to be several caves in the cliff, dominates the skyline. This is Pontatoc Ridge. The Pontatoc Ridge Trail ends to the right of the largest opening in the cliff, which is actually an abandoned mine. The following description is purposely detailed. Follow it carefully, and you will be rewarded with a great hike that provides dramatic views of Tucson. In addition, you'll get a better understanding of the early mining history of the Catalinas.

You may feel like a mouse wandering through a maze in search of cheese on the lower section of this trail! Several false trails lead off to the right and are tempting to take because they appear to head directly

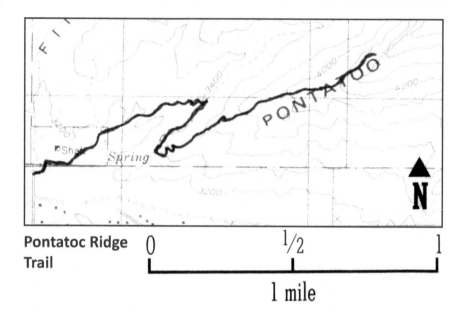

Pontatoc Ridge Trail   0   1/2   1

1 mile

for the ridge, but remember to keep bearing slightly to the left, heading for the cliff. The last time I hiked this trail, side trails had been blocked off by rows of rocks which, hopefully, have not been disturbed.

After about 0.6 of a mile, the trail drops into a small drainage, comes out, and descends into another somewhat deeper drainage. Shortly you come to a third drainage that is deep and very pronounced. This is the lower part of Pontatoc Canyon. If there has been adequate rainfall, there may be water running. At any time of year there is an assortment of wildflowers that makes this a pretty spot.

It is a steep climb out of the drainage, and you enter an area that is covered with amole (shindaggers), those spearlike plants that attack you at shin level. The vegetation is mostly palo verde and mesquite trees, prickly pear, cholla and barrel cacti, and ocotillos. There is not a very thick stand of saguaros on this trail, unlike most of the trails of the front range.

As you go up the switchbacks, turn right at a signed intersection on the Pontatoc Ridge Trail, which quickly levels off along the side of the ridge. This is a pleasant part of the trail, with excellent views of the

Pontatoc Ridge.

west side of Tucson and of Finger Rock. As you round the ridge, the entire city spreads out below.

There is a large, flat, rocky area that is a good spot to have lunch or just relax. If you are careful, this spot is excellent for a hike during a full moon. A perfect scenario is to hike up right before sunset, watch the sun go down, the moon rise, and the lights of the city come on as you enjoy a picnic dinner!

For about a half mile the trail is again hard to follow. There are cairns that mark the general direction, but, should they be gone, remember to bear to the left slightly and continue up the ridge. There are several steep step-ups. One section looks like someone deliberately planted teddy bear cholla, and, for about a quarter mile, you have to be very careful not to bump into one, or you will learn why they are called "jumping" cactus.

Beyond the cholla, for about a half mile, the trail is a slab of rock, and it is again easy to stray off the trail. There is a large rock outcropping so the best route is to go to the left. Watch carefully for rows of rocks that block the side trails. There are times when it appears that you should go to the right, when most of the time the trail is actually to the left. If you do get off the trail, it is not disastrous, and you will wander back on the correct path.

You continue to climb gradually for about three-quarters of a mile, occasionally encountering a few minor switchbacks, including one set that goes to the right. The views as you crest the ridge are spectacular. Below, you can see where the Pontatoc Canyon Trail switchbacks out of the canyon.

From this point the Pontatoc Ridge Trail is distinct, as it makes its way to the mine area. Very shortly you come to a saddle. To the right of the trail are excellent views of the east side of Tucson. You look down on the Skyline Country Club and the homes of the Skyline Country Club Estates.

Past the saddle the trail becomes steeper and is quite rocky. As you get closer to the ridge, there is more evidence of mining activity, and the openings in the cliff are clearly visible. A sign indicates the end of the Pontatoc Ridge Trail. It is dangerous to proceed beyond this point.

Finger Rock Trail

General Description: A steep climb through a beautiful canyon with spectacular views

Difficulty: Extremely difficult, steep, continuous climbing after the first mile

Best Time of Year to Hike: Spring and Fall

Length: 10 miles round-trip

Miles to Trailhead from Speedway/Campbell Intersection: 8.4 miles

Directions to Trailhead from Speedway/Campbell Intersection: Go north on Campbell Avenue 6.2 miles to Skyline Drive. Turn right on Skyline Drive for 0.5 of a mile. At this point Skyline divides and turns left. Continue on Skyline for 0.7 of a mile to the intersection of Alvernon Way. Turn left on Alvernon Way, which dead-ends. The Richard "Dick" McKee Trailhead parking area is on the left. Turn in carefully, avoiding the wrong way spikes.

■ ■ ■

A dominant landmark of the Catalinas is Finger Rock, a tall rock spire that points skyward about midway through the range. It is possible to get a better view of that rock spire by climbing the Finger Rock Trail to Mount Kimball, through some of the most spectacular scenery in the Catalinas.

The well-marked trail begins to the right of a sign at the end of the street. After an initial short climb, the trail is basically level for 1.1 miles. The trail heads into Finger Rock Canyon, through an impressive stand of saguaros. The spring, usually a permanent water source, empties

141

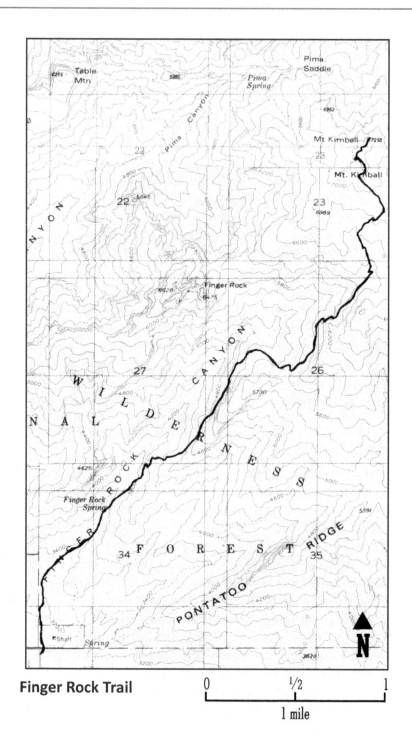

Finger Rock Trail

0   ¹/₂   1

1 mile

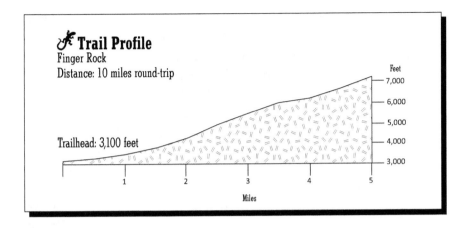

🦎 Trail Profile
Finger Rock
Distance: 10 miles round-trip

Trailhead: 3,100 feet

Feet
7,000
6,000
5,000
4,000
3,000

Miles

into a partially covered concrete tank to the left of the trail. Do not follow the trail that continues level beyond the spring, unless you want to spend some time in the canyon bottom.

The Finger Rock Trail switchbacks to the right, up the side of the canyon. As you work your way up the switchbacks, Finger Rock appears larger; however, this is as close as the trail comes to the actual rock formation. This initial climb up the switchbacks is one of the hardest parts of the trail, with steep step-ups and several areas of loose rock.

After the switchbacks, the trail drops into a small drainage. This section has many amoles and it is important to stay on the trail to avoid being punctured in the shins by the sharp spines of the plant. The trail continues to climb around the canyon basin. There are no parts of the Finger Rock Trail that could be called easy. In fact, except for a few very short sections, the Finger Rock Trail is relentless in its climb to Mount Kimball. The views are excellent, however, and always worth the climb.

After about two miles you reach a large, flat rock on the left, overlooking the canyon. You have gained enough elevation that the saguaros have disappeared and have been replaced by piñon pine, juniper, and several varieties of oak. Finger Rock is now obscured by the cliffs and will not be visible for the remainder of the hike.

There are some places in this portion of the trail that can be confusing. There is a side trail to Linda Vista Saddle to the right that leads to an overlook of the city, but it involves some very steep, unnecessary climbing. Wait a few hundred yards for a second trail to the right that will get you to the saddle with very little effort.

Before reaching this second trail to the right, you will see a distinct trail to the left. Even though this trail is blocked by a row of small rocks, it looks like the logical trail to take to Mount Kimball, and many hikers mistakenly head in this direction. Don't! Continue on the main trail, which bears to the right. On this main trail, and immediately after a short steep section, a spur trail goes to the right and is the correct route to reach Linda Vista Saddle. The spur trail is level except for a brief climb at the end.

Linda Vista means beautiful view, and that's exactly what the area provides. From the saddle, you can see the entire Tucson Valley. Westin La Paloma Resort looks like a pink dollhouse below. This is a good turn-around spot if you want a short hike. It takes about two and a half hours to hike the three miles to the saddle.

If you choose to continue the remaining two miles to Mount Kimball, expect some steep climbing ahead. Take the spur trail from Linda Vista Saddle back to the main trail and continue around the basin. Several varieties of oak shade the trail, and you pass beneath huge boulders. Mistletoe hangs from most of the trees. For a short period the trail is smooth, but it soon becomes rocky again. Baboquivari Peak, Kitt Peak, and most of the west side of the city, including downtown Tucson and the white buildings of the Arizona Health Sciences Center, are visible from here.

The scenery in this section is dramatic, with stark cliffs towering above the tall pines. The carpet of soft pine needles is quite a treat after the rocky trail. There are several excellent camping spots and two small drainages that are likely to have water during winter and early spring.

Past the pines, you come to a more open area, covered with manzanitas and small oaks. The city spreads out below and the views are great, but, unfortunately, pine needles yield to rocks again.

As you begin to top out, you come to a small saddle and a directional sign. Turn left on the Pima Canyon Trail, Number 62. Past the sign the trail turns north and once again begins to climb through piñon pine and juniper. Soon you are again hiking under tall pines, and this is a lovely portion of the hike. Follow the trail along the crest to the right for about 200 yards, and you will come to a large, flat rock outcropping

Hiker studies saguaro on the Finger Rock Trail.

that is an excellent lunch spot and lookout. Depending on your conditioning, it will take four to five hours to reach Mount Kimball and almost as long to return.

To use an old hiking cliché, the views are worth every step. The Finger Rock Trail takes you to the heart of the Catalinas. Cathedral Rock and Mount Lemmon are to the east. You can see part of Pusch Ridge to the west; Picacho Peak and Sun City Tucson are to the northwest; and, almost due north, you can see the white structures of Biosphere II.

Most who hike to the summit of Mount Kimball would be surprised to learn that the peak was named for an early developer—Frederick E. A. Kimball. Kimball moved to Tucson in 1899 and lived here until his death in 1930. He was one of the first property owners in Summerhaven and, during the summers, served as postmaster of the tiny village. He urged the building of a short road to Mount Lemmon and promoted the development of Summerhaven as a summer recreation area. At the time of his death, Kimball was secretary-treasurer of the Summerhaven Land and Improvement Company.

In addition to his interest in Summerhaven, Kimball owned a printing business and a book and stationery store in Tucson. At one time he was a reporter for the *Arizona Daily Star*. He served four terms in the Arizona legislature and, at the time of his death, was in the state senate. As senator, Kimball secured passage of the state's first child welfare bill and supported the establishment of the Catalina Game Preserve.

An ardent outdoorsman, Kimball was a member of the Game Protective Association and an organizer of the Tucson Natural History Society. It was this group that appealed to the United States Geographic Board (USGB) for the naming of a peak in the Catalinas in his memory. The previously unnamed peak was officially designated as Mount Kimball by the USGB on February 4, 1931.

Although Kimball spent much time hiking in the Catalinas in the area around Summerhaven, it is not known whether he ever stood atop the peak that was named after him. It is certain that he would have been pleased with the choice.

Pima Canyon Trail

General Description: A long hike through a beautiful canyon into one of the most rugged areas of the Catalina Mountains

Difficulty: Difficult, easy for first 3.2 miles

Best Time of Year to Hike: Early spring, late fall

Length: 14.2 miles round-trip

Miles to Trailhead from Speedway/Campbell Intersection: 10 miles

Directions to Trailhead from Speedway/Campbell Intersection: Go north on Campbell for 5.4 miles to Skyline Drive. Turn left on Skyline and continue to Ina Road. Continue on Ina until you reach Christie Drive. Follow Christie Drive north until it dead-ends at Magee Road. Turn right on Magee, and you will see the Iris O. Dewhirst Trailhead parking area straight ahead and on the right. Watch carefully to avoid wrong way spikes.

■ ■ ■

The Pima Canyon Trail is one of the most popular trails in the front range of the Santa Catalina Mountains. It is easily accessible, not too difficult for the first three miles, and beautiful. Beginning in 1996, the US Forest Service instituted new regulations to protect the dwindling bighorn sheep herd believed to inhabit the upper reaches of Pima Canyon. From January through April, the new regulations included restricting any off-trail hiking or camping beyond 400 feet of authorized trails and limiting day hiking groups to fifteen and overnight parties to six. Dogs are forbidden on any part of the trail. The regulations were not successful and, as of this printing, there are no bighorn sheep left in the Catalinas.

147

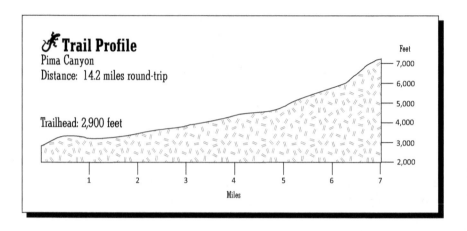

🦎 Trail Profile

Pima Canyon
Distance: 14.2 miles round-trip

Trailhead: 2,900 feet

Feet

7,000
6,000
5,000
4,000
3,000
2,000

Miles

The trail leaves from the east corner of the trailhead parking lot, past a plaque placed on a boulder in memory of Tom Bingham. Bingham loved hiking the Pima Canyon Trail and was instrumental in securing unrestricted public access to the trail, which crosses private property before entering the Coronado National Forest. Bingham fell to his death on April 12, 1992, while rock climbing by himself in Pima Canyon.

Past the plaque, interpretive signs introduce hikers to Pima Canyon. The first 0.75 mile crosses private land through a fenced corridor before entering the national forest and climbing to the base of the mountains. The vegetation is typical of the 2,500- to 3,200-foot elevations of the Sonoran Desert—saguaro, prickly pear, barrel, and cholla cacti, catclaw, ocotillo, brittlebush, mesquite, and palo verde. The views of Tucson from this section show the entire valley. South, the 9,453-foot peak of Mount Wrightson is clearly visible, as is the *A* on "A" Mountain. Far to the west, Baboquivari Peak, sacred mountain of the Tohono O'odham Indians, and the Kitt Peak Observatory are the dominant landmarks.

After about a mile of easy hiking with some brief climbing, the trail drops sharply into the creek bed. The creek is dry much of the year, but is lovely when it is flowing, mostly in winter and spring.

As you cross the creek and round a curve, the city disappears. This is one of the joys of living in Tucson and having the Catalinas in your backyard. Within an hour of hiking, you can escape the city. The trail parallels the stream for the next two miles, occasionally crossing to the

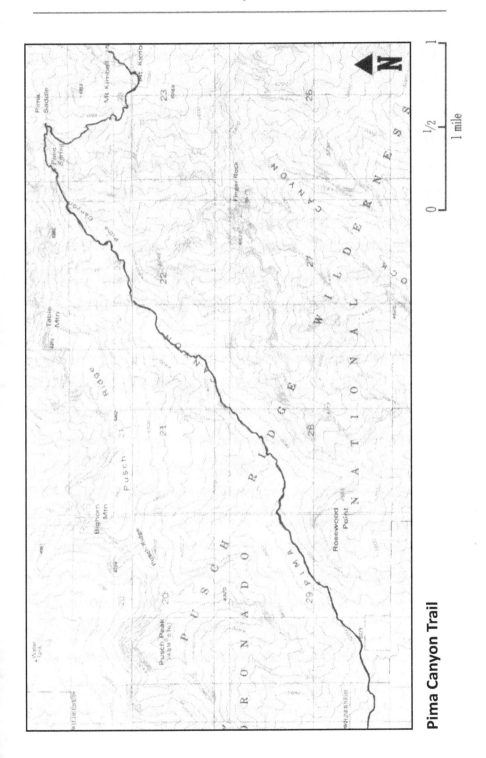

other side. Even when the stream is running, it is easy to boulder-hop across. A half mile into the canyon, the first cottonwoods appear. Soon the giant trees provide a canopy, and you are walking in the shade. This is one of the prettiest areas on the lower portion of the Pima Canyon Trail.

As you leave the dense trees, the canyon opens up. The drainage from Pusch Ridge comes in from the north. Here the trail becomes confusing, crossing the narrow streambed several times. If you are in doubt as to the correct route of the trail, stop, look for cairns indicating direction, or rows of rocks blocking the wrong way. The ascent into the canyon becomes slightly more difficult. After a particularly steep, but mercifully short, climb, you'll know you are nearing the Pima Canyon Dam. You will cross several large slabs of rock right before the dam.

The Pima Canyon Dam was built by the Arizona Game and Fish Division as a source of water for wildlife. This is a good lunch spot. Secluded in a bend of the canyon, you would never know that a city of nearly two million people was only three miles away. Flowers cling to the drainage around the dam. Birds chatter and occasionally dive down for a drink. It is no wonder that in an earlier time, around A.D. 1000, this spot was home to the Hohokam Indians. Two hundred yards to the left of the dam as you face down the canyon are bedrock mortars, depressions in the rock formed by Indian women grinding mesquite beans. Two mortars are very deep, and there are several smaller ones nearby. It is easy to imagine Indian women sitting on the rocks, chatting, and grinding beans, while their men hunted.

It takes the average hiker about two hours to reach this point. You have hiked three miles and gained 800 feet in elevation, from 2,900 feet at the trailhead to 3,700 feet at the dam. The dam is a short side trip; the trail continues across a rock slab and away from the dam. This first portion of the trail is an excellent introduction to the canyons of the Catalinas and is a good turnaround spot for a beginning hiker.

A lot more is ahead if you choose to continue up the canyon. For another mile the elevation gain is gradual. The saguaros disappear and are replaced by Mexican blue oaks. The trail crosses one of the loveliest spots in Pima Canyon. For about a mile the trail is high above the creek. A bit farther and you cross large slabs of rock, interspersed with pools of water. To the right is a dam, this one larger than the first.

Hikers on the Pima Canyon Trail.

Beyond this dam, the trail begins to climb sharply. You are headed into one of the most rugged sections of the Catalinas and one of the most dramatically beautiful.

You climb continually for another mile until you reach Pima Canyon Spring. At the spring you will have come 5.2 miles from the trailhead and gained 2,550 feet in elevation. This spring provides a permanent source of water. As you approach the spring there are two concrete tanks, which, as you will see shortly, are connected by pipe to a spring above. There are several good campsites around the spring area.

Above the spring you have to be a serious, well-conditioned hiker to continue. Study the map carefully to get an indication of what is ahead. Mount Kimball is at 7,200 feet, you are at 5,550 feet. It is a rough 1.9-mile climb to the summit.

As you leave the canyon from the spring, you climb sharply along an open hillside. The views of the city to the south and of the canyon to the north are awesome. As you're looking up the canyon, actually climbing it doesn't seem possible.

A half mile into the climb, you come to a small sign pointing to Pima Saddle. A short spur trail leads to the saddle, and if you have time, the views are worth it. You get a glimpse of the "other side of the moun-tain." Between this sign and Mount Kimball is some of the most difficult climbing and trail finding in the Catalinas. As my hiking companion said, "There are one hundred places you can break your leg," and, a few minutes later, I heard, "This is the worst trail I have ever been on!" The trail bears to the right around a large rock outcropping. Although there are numerous cairns that lead straight up the drainage, the trail goes to the right, and shortly becomes more defined.

Despite the difficulty, in terms of scenery and views the trip up the canyon and to Mount Kimball is, for want of a better word, spectacular. How many people can say they have seen the back of Finger Rock? As you near Mount Kimball, ponderosa pines tower above you. You feel like you are on top of the world. Look north, and you see Biosphere II near Oracle, to the east is Mount Lemmon, look south and all of Tucson spreads out below.

The trip up and down the Pima Canyon Trail requires the entire day. Depending on your conditioning, I would estimate at least six hours up and five hours back, allowing reasonable time for resting and enjoying the views from the top. An interesting variation is to come up the Pima Canyon Trail and descend by way of the shorter Finger Rock Trail. This requires leaving a vehicle at each trailhead, but will shorten the return trip.

Box Camp Trail

General Description: An excellent hike, beginning in pines and ending in saguaro cacti that, with a car shuttle, is nearly all downhill

Difficulty: Difficult, mostly continuous steep downhill

Best Time of Year to Hike: Spring, fall

Length: 9.6 miles one way to Sabino Canyon Tram

Miles to Trailhead from Speedway/Campbell Intersection: 32.9 miles from intersection to trailhead (does not include leaving a car at Sabino Canyon Visitor Center parking lot)

Directions to Trailhead from Speedway/Campbell Intersection: Leave one car at the Sabino Canyon Visitor Center parking lot. Go east on Speedway to Wilmot Road. Turn left on Wilmot Road. Wilmot becomes Tanque Verde. Continue on Tanque Verde until Sabino Canyon Road. Turn left on Sabino Canyon Road and continue until you reach the Visitor Center parking lot, which is on the right. Get in the second car and go back to Tanque Verde. Turn left and drive until you reach the Catalina Highway. Turn left on the Catalina Highway until 0.8 of a mile past Milepost 21. The parking area for the Box Camp Trail is on the left, past Spencer Canyon Road and before Milepost 22. (This car shuttle can be avoided if you can talk someone into driving you up to the trailhead.)

■ ■ ■

The Box Camp Trail, built by Frank Webber in 1897, was the first pack route to the high country of the Santa Catalina Mountains. In the days before air-conditioning Tucsonans rode horses up this trail to summer cabins or camps to escape the heat. Hunters established a camp in the pines high on a ridge where they nailed boxes to the trees to protect their food supplies, hence the name Box Camp.

The trail, which today connects the Catalina Highway to the Sabino Canyon tram, is one of the most dramatic trails in the Tucson area. The trail begins at 8,050 feet and, after 7.1 miles of nearly continuous downhill hiking, ends in Sabino Basin at 3,700 feet. From Sabino Basin it is 2.5 miles to the head of the Sabino Canyon Road, where, if you choose, you can catch the tram to the visitor center parking lot.

The trail starts up the hill to the right of the parking area and climbs about 200 yards before leveling out. Unfortunately much of the upper portion of the trail was devasted by forest fires. The once large pine trees that shaded the trail are now black trunks. The trail continues along the bottom of a ravine, crossing and recrossing the small stream several times. There is nearly always water in early spring. The trail continues down for another quarter mile before emerging from the burned forest into a more open area with small oaks and manzanita. From here on, the views of the city and the nearby canyons are awesome. Notice Thimble Peak, the prominent thimble-shaped landmark above Sabino Canyon. Before your hike is over, you will be looking up at the Thimble.

The now-rocky trail goes down the top of the ridge between Spencer Canyon on the left and Box Camp Canyon on the right. The trail crosses this cleared area and continues down the mountain. There has by now been an almost total change in vegetation. An hour ago you were in what remained of a pine forest. Now you are hiking through manzanita, oak, and piñon pine.

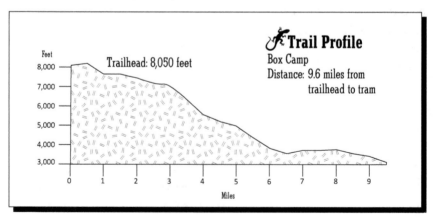

Trail Profile

Box Camp
Distance: 9.6 miles from
          trailhead to tram

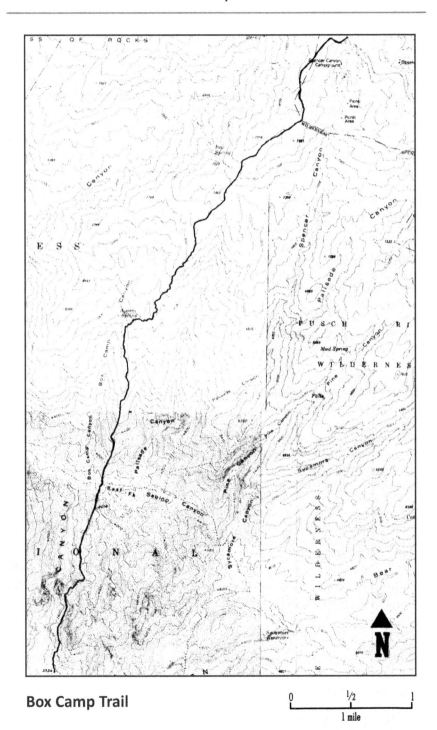

Box Camp Trail

0   ½   1
1 mile

Look carefully for cairns and avoid side trails that are blocked by a row of rocks. The trail goes basically straight for about half a mile before bearing to the right or northwest. As you continue to descend, the trail switchbacks steeply down through loose rocks before leveling out in a brushy area.

The trail approaches Box Camp Canyon and then turns left, or southeast, and circles the ridge. In about a mile, an interesting rock formation comes into view. It is a long, high sheaf of rocks that has many balanced rocks on top. This is the area known as Apache Spring. The trail crosses a small stream, and there are some large pines to provide shade. Most of the year there will be at least a little water and a number of wildflowers growing in this area. It is easy to understand why the native American Indians chose this location for their camp.

Across the stream and on top of a large flat rock to the right you'll find bowl shaped depressions called metates made by Hohokam women grinding mesquite beans. Another large rock at the base of the sheaf of rocks also has several metates. Imagine the scene hundreds of years ago when women ground mesquite beans on these rocks while the men hunted and the children scrambled in the rock formations.

The trail changes in character as it switchbacks its way down through an area covered with large boulders. There are some pine trees and a number of large oaks, breaking for a while the intense sun of the previous part of the trail.

After coming out of this boulder-strewn section, you are close to Box Camp Canyon. Watch carefully for a sharp turn to the right, where the correct route switchbacks steeply down before making a sharp left and turning toward Sabino Canyon. After descending the switchbacks, the trail circles the ridge and provides a good view of Palisades Canyon, where, if there is enough water, there is a large waterfall. At one point the trail appears to head back uphill and toward the mountains. Don't worry! It soon makes a sharp right and heads directly for Sabino Basin through a short, level area.

This section is more open with an abundance of the nastiest plant in the Catalinas—amole, better known as shindaggers. A series of switchbacks weaves through the shindaggers directly to Sabino Basin. Here the saguaros appear again and by now you are at about the 3,500-foot level.

Hikers pause to take in the view on the Box Camp Trail.

At the bottom of the switchbacks, you level off briefly and then enter the cool, shady Sabino Basin. Work your way across the creek to the intersection of the Box Camp and East Fork of Sabino Trails. Turn right a few hundred yards to a major trail intersection. Follow Sabino Canyon Trail Number 23 across the creek and out of the basin.

The trail climbs steeply out of Sabino Basin for the first half mile and then circles the canyon for approximately 1.5 miles until coming to the switchbacks that look down on the road. This is the route to the paved road. Sometimes it seems to me that this last half mile of switchbacks down to the tram is the longest portion of the trail! When the tram arrives, give the driver $8 and hop on board unless you prefer to walk.

Invariably, since you obviously look a little worse for wear, someone will say, "Where did you come from?" It is fun to see their reaction when you say, "Mount Lemmon!"

Romero Canyon Trail

General Description: A hike to a canyon with deep year-round pools suitable for swimming

Difficulty: Moderate, some areas of steep climbing

Best Time of Year to Hike: Spring, fall, winter

Length: 5.6 miles round-trip

Miles to Trailhead from Speedway/Campbell Intersection: 15.7 miles

Directions to Trailhead from Speedway/Campbell Intersection: Go north on Campbell Avenue 6.2 miles to Skyline Drive. Turn left on Skyline Drive and take it to Oracle Road. Turn right on Oracle and continue north to the entrance of Catalina State Park. Drive to the trailhead parking area at the end of the road. The Romero Canyon Trailhead is to the right, past the bulletin board and rest rooms.

Fees: Entry fees to Catalina State Park are $7 per vehicle with 1 to 4 persons. Individuals entering the park on foot pay $3.

■ ■ ■

Romero Canyon is a spectacular canyon on the north side of the Santa Catalina Mountains. The Romero Canyon Trail leads into the mountains and connects with the West Fork of Sabino Trail, enabling the adventurous hiker to cross the mountains into Sabino Canyon, or, by intersecting with the Mount Lemmon Trail, to climb to the summit of Mount Lemmon. This trail description is for the first 2.8 miles of the Romero Canyon Trail, the portion that leads to an area known as Romero Pools.

The pools and canyon are named after Fabian Romero, who,

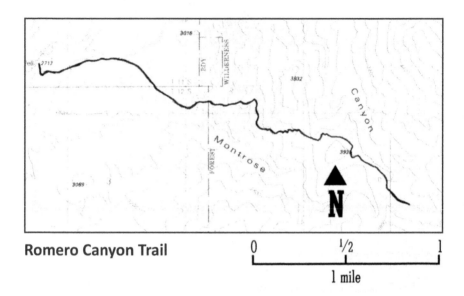

Romero Canyon Trail   0   ½   1

1 mile

in 1889, established Rancho Romero in Canada del Oro, near where Oracle Junction is today. The ranch, the first in that area, covered 4,800 acres.

The trail into Romero Canyon leaves across from the parking lot and immediately crosses Canada del Oro Wash. If there has been adequate rainfall or snowmelt, the wash is running, and you must boulder-hop or wade across. Once across the wash, the trail climbs immediately to the East. A newly constructed wide sandy path climbs the hill. At the top of the first rise is a level area where two benches provide a good spot to sit, rest, and view the riparian area below.

The trail continues southeast to the intersection of the Canyon Loop Trail and the Romero Canyon Trail. The Canyon Loop Trail is a pleasant 2.5-mile loop trail that connects with the Sutherland Trail to return to the parking area. The Romero Canyon Trail continues straight ahead and is level and sandy and wide enough to be a road. It passes through a large stand of mesquite and heads directly for the base of the mountains. After one quarter of a mile, another intersection is reached, that of Romero and Montrose Canyons. Montrose Canyon is a deep canyon to the west with several large pools. A steep trail leads down into the canyon. The trail is not maintained and a sign warns,

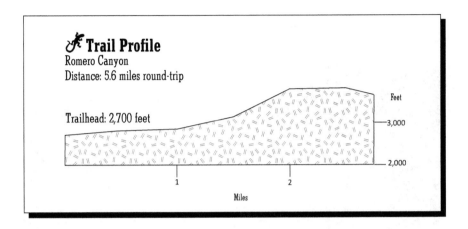

⚹ Trail Profile

Romero Canyon

Distance: 5.6 miles round-trip

Trailhead: 2,700 feet

"Danger—Unsafe Footing Beyond this Point."

The Romero Canyon Trail climbs to the left of the intersection and immediately becomes narrow and rocky. At the National Forest Boundary sign, hikers are warned that dogs are not permitted beyond this point. The trail climbs steadily, and the views of both the valley and the mountains are excellent. This is a heavily used trail, and many hikers have made side trails leading to lookout points, which may temporarily cause you to stray off the trail. Also, the trail occasionally splits, but always returns to the main trail, making whichever direction you take all right. For the most part the trail is clearly marked, and there is no question as to the route.

The trail circles the drainage, gradually climbing toward the crest of the ridge. The vegetation is diverse in the shelter of the drainage. Small saguaros are thriving under their "nurse" trees. In spring the wildflowers are profuse. The entire area is a jumble of boulders.

As the trail continues to climb, it goes through a slit in the rock and then seriously begins climbing toward the crest of a ridge. A series of steep, rocky switchbacks brings you to the top of the ridge. There are several places where the trail has been shortcut, a hiking term that means that hikers have cut across a switchback, going straight up the trail rather than using the switchback. Shortcutting causes erosion and is not good hiking etiquette. Unfortunately, any trail that is used by a great number of people attracts many who are not concerned about

Romero Pools.

the effects of their actions on the environment. In a few years this section of the trail will be badly eroded unless preventive maintenance is done.

The views of the Santa Catalinas from the ridge are spectacular in this area, and you realize you are entering rugged country. From the crest of this first ridge, the trail descends briefly and crosses a saddle between two ridges. To the left, after about 0.2 of a mile, you get your first view of Romero Canyon. There is a large waterfall at the base of the canyon. It appears as if it is possible to climb down to the waterfall from this point, but the route is treacherous, and it is better to work your way down farther along the trail and nearer the creek.

Fortunately the trail does not climb the steep ridge in front of you but circles it to the northeast. This portion of the trail, shaded by tall oak trees, is especially beautiful, with the views of the canyon on the left. As the trail drops into Romero Canyon, you can see the area called Romero Pools. It takes the average hiker two to two and a half hours to reach the pool area. The trail crosses the stream, and from there it is possible to boulder-hop to the several pools that continue downstream. Less than a quarter of a mile upstream you'll find another series of pools.

Hirabayashi Recreation Site to Sabino Canyon

General Description: An easy walk, mostly downhill, from an old prison camp, now called the Gordon Hirabayashi Recreation Site, to Sabino Canyon

Difficulty: Moderate

Best Time of Year to Hike: Winter, early spring, late fall

Length: 7.6 miles one way

Miles to Trailhead from Speedway/Campbell Intersection: 20.4 miles

Directions to Trailhead from Speedway/Campbell Intersection: This hike requires two vehicles. The ideal way is to leave your vehicle at the Sabino Canyon Visitor Center parking lot and have a friend drive you to the Gordon Hirabayashi Recreation Site on the Catalina Highway. Drive east on Speedway Boulevard to the intersection of Wilmot Road. Turn left on Wilmot. Wilmot Road becomes Tanque Verde Road at the intersection of Pima and Wilmot. Continue on Tanque Verde Road to Sabino Canyon Road. Turn left on Sabino Canyon Road and leave a vehicle at the Sabino Canyon Visitor Center parking lot. Retrace your route on Sabino Canyon Road to Tanque Verde. Turn left on Tanque Verde Road to the Catalina Highway. Turn left on Catalina Highway and drive 0.4 of a mile past Milepost 7, where an intersection sign indicates a paved road to the left. Turn on this road and drive 200 yards to a paved parking area near the end of the loop and on the right. This is the Gordon Hirabayashi Recreation Site and the starting point of the hike.

■ ■ ■

I f you want to be somewhat poetic, tell friends you are hiking from the dam to the tram! We'll leave the parking lot of the Gordon Hirabayashi Recreation Site, hike to Sycamore Dam, and end up at Stop 9 of the Sabino Canyon Tram, where $8 will get you a ride to our waiting car.

Only the foundations remain of what was once a large prison camp. The camp resulted from efforts of *Tucson Citizen* editor Frank Harris Hitchcock, who, in the early 1930s, tried to get a road built to Mount Lemmon. When two bond issues failed, General Hitchcock, as he was known from his term as Postmaster General of the United States, convinced an old Washington friend, Stanford Bates, Director of the Federal Bureau of Prisons, to supply prison labor for construction of the road, thus transferring funding for the project to the federal government.

Construction began on a permanent camp to house the prisoners at Vail Corral Basin, near today's Gordon Hirabayashi Recreation Site. When finally completed in February of 1939, the camp had a total of fifty-five buildings, including barracks, a kitchen, mess hall, a power and steam heating plant, laundry, training shop, garage, and housing for officers and guards.

The General Hitchcock Highway, as it was officially named, received final inspection on February 28, 1951. Prison records show that 8,003 inmates were assigned to the Tucson Prison Camp during road construction. The twenty-five miles of road cost an average of $4,000 per mile. The Prison Camp remained open until 1967, when the Bureau of Prisons closed the camp because of the high cost of operation. In 1973 the Forest Service razed the abandoned buildings.

The site of the prison camp is now called the Gordon Hirabayashi Recreation Site, named in honor of a Japanese-American interred here during World War II. The trail begins at the lower end of the campground. A trail sign on the left indicates Sycamore Reservoir Trail #39. Follow the directional arrow to the top of the hill where another trail sign indicates that the Sycamore Reservoir Trail #39 turns to the right.

After a brief downhill stretch, the trail, which is part of the official Arizona Trail, begins to climb into a saddle, where a large sign depicts the route of the Arizona Trail. Now closed to vehicles, the road on the right was the supply road to the Sycamore Reservoir. Your route is to

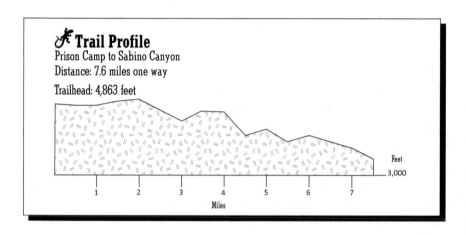

follow the Sycamore Reservoir Trail #39 on the left. It is a mile from this sign to the dam.

As you begin switchbacking down the trail, look on the left for several pillars of varying heights, the tallest being about five feet. These were the supports that carried the pipeline that brought utility water from the reservoir to the prison camp. As you near the dam, the trail veers right and for a short time joins the road that led to the dam. A path goes off to the right at the bottom of the hill. This will be our eventual route, but for now continue straight ahead and take a look at the dam. You pass a concrete slab that once held the pump house for the dam.

When the prison camp was in operation, this dam backed up a large reservoir. Even today it is a massive structure and water usually roars over the spillway. When you tire of looking at the dam, it's time to head for the tram. You are headed for Sycamore Canyon, the first canyon to the right as you look down the spillway of the dam. To get to the trail, you must make a loop to avoid the water and dense vegetation near the dam. Leave the platform and follow the path back in the direction of the trail. The path veers to the left and follows the base of a hill for about 100 yards before turning sharply to the left and crossing into Sycamore Canyon. The correct route has been marked by a series of large cairns.

After crossing the creek, the trail becomes distinct and begins to climb gradually. For about a half mile the trail follows the creek bed and is rocky. Watch carefully for when the trail leaves the creek bed,

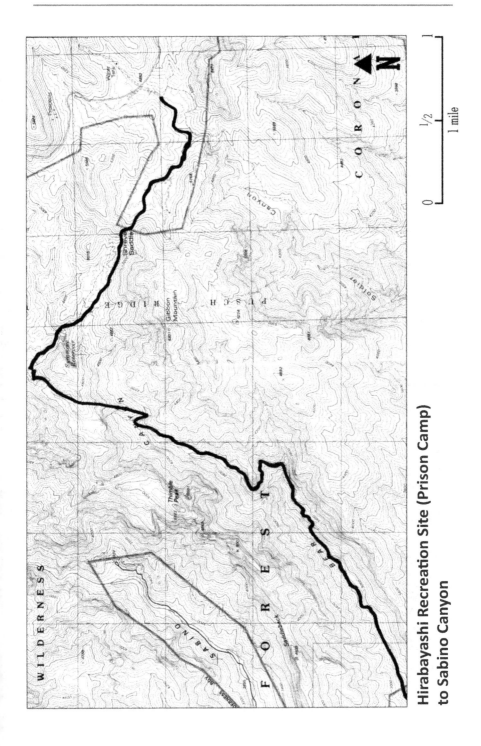

Hirabayashi Recreation Site (Prison Camp)
to Sabino Canyon

Sycamore Dam.

and bears to the right. As it does, the trail begins to climb more steeply, goes through a thick stand of manzanitas, and becomes more open. In summer, this portion of the trail is deadly, but in winter, it is a perfect hike. The trail drops and crosses the creek, then climbs out of the creek, winds to the left, and begins to climb to a saddle. Right before the saddle, the Bear Canyon Trail turns to the left. Sycamore Reservoir Trail #39 ends at this intersection, and you now join East Fork Trail #24A, which bears to the right and leads into Sabino Basin.

The East Fork Trail switchbacks sharply down toward Sabino Basin and is a spectacular section of trail. Across the canyon, you see the switchbacks of the Palisades Trail as it comes down from the Palisades Ranger Station. There are some steep drop-offs, and you have to watch for loose rocks, but for the most part, this is a well-marked and maintained trail. As the trail reaches Sabino Creek, a sign indicates the intersection of the Palisades and East Fork Trails. Continue on the East Fork Trail, paralleling the stream for much of the way. The trail comes out into the open before circling back and rejoining the creek bed.

You quickly come to a major trail intersection having several signs to direct the hiker. Since you are headed for the tram, your route is to cross the creek and follow the Sabino Canyon Trail for 2.5 miles out of the basin. It quickly switchbacks away from the creek and offers great views of the basin and the Santa Catalina Mountains. As you top the final ridge, you can see the road and usually the tram approaching. Partway down the final switchbacks, the Phoneline Trail cuts off to the left. If you are feeling particularly ambitious, you can follow this trail out of the canyon. Should you opt for the tram, give the driver $8, climb on board, and relax.

Hutch's Pool

General Description: A pleasant hike to one of the most beautiful pools in the Catalinas

Difficulty: Moderate, steep switchbacks for first 0.8 of a mile

Best Time of Year to Hike: Early spring, late fall, winter

Length: 8.2 miles round-trip using the tram

Miles to Trailhead from Speedway/Campbell Intersection: 11.1 miles

Directions to Trailhead from Speedway/Campbell: Go east on Speedway 5 miles to Wilmot Road. Turn left. Wilmot becomes Tanque Verde at the Pima intersection. Continue on Tanque Verde to Sabino Canyon Road. Turn left and follow the signs to the Sabino Canyon Visitor Center parking lot. The trailhead is at the end of Sabino Canyon Road, 3.8 miles from the Visitor Center. You may walk up the road or take the Sabino Canyon tram to the end of the road.

Fees: The fee to park in Sabino Canyon is $5 per day. The America the Beautiful cards, which are $80 for an Annual Pass, $10 for a lifetime Senior Pass, and free of charge for an Access Pass available to permanently disabled US citizens, are also accepted as is the Coronado Recreation Pass, which is $5 for a daily pass, $10 for a weekly pass, and $20 for an annual pass. Both cards are available for purchase at the Sabino Canyon Visitor Center. Put the card on the dashboard of your vehicle.

■   ■   ■

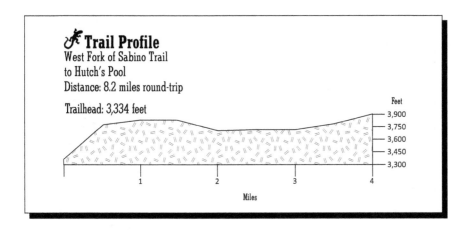

Trail Profile
West Fork of Sabino Trail
to Hutch's Pool
Distance: 8.2 miles round-trip

Trailhead: 3,334 feet

In the early 1940s Don Everett, English and Latin teacher at the Southern Arizona School for Boys (now Fenster School of Arizona), took his students on horseback rides into the Santa Catalina Mountains. Whenever he would pass a prominent landmark for the first time, Everett would name it after a student in his group. On a ride from Sabino Canyon to Mount Lemmon, Everett passed what he called "the most beautiful pool in the Catalinas." A student from Chicago, Roger Hutchinson, was on the ride, and Everett named the pool Hutch's Pool.

The switchbacks at the north end of Sabino Canyon Road are the starting point for several trails leading into the Santa Catalinas, including the West Fork of Sabino Trail, which passes Hutch's Pool. The quickest way to reach the trailhead is by the Sabino Canyon tram ($8 per person) but some hardy hikers prefer to walk the additional 3.8 miles to the switchbacks.

However you choose to traverse Sabino Canyon, you will agree that it is a rare oasis in the desert. No one knows for certain how Sabino Canyon got its name. David Wentworth Lazaroff, in his excellent book, *Sabino Canyon: The Life of a Southwestern Oasis*, theorizes that the name was applied by early Spanish-speaking visitors, who often named places in Arizona after trees. He writes, "In Mexico sabino is a name applied to small-fruited conifers such as bald cypress or juniper. The best candidate in Sabino Canyon is a beautiful tree called the Arizona cypress." He explains that although today only a few small cypress grow

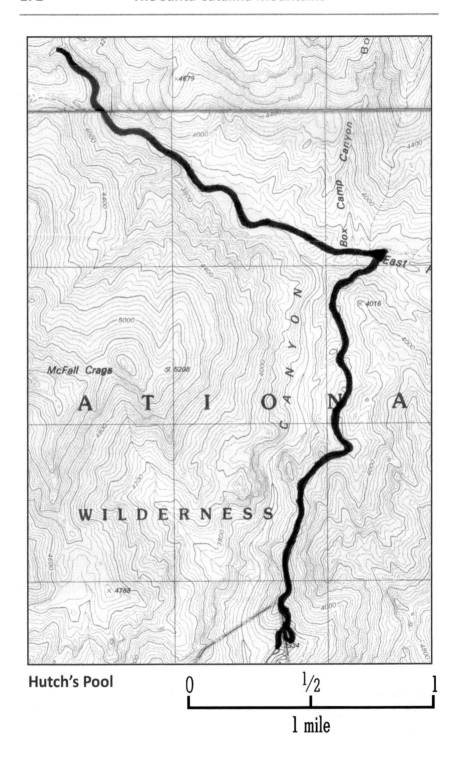

Hutch's Pool

0   1/2   1

1 mile

Hutch's Pool.

in the canyon, two hundred years ago the climate was wetter, and perhaps several large cypress grew near the mouth of the canyon, thus the name sabino, or cypress.

The trail to Hutch's Pool begins at the end of the road on the Sabino Canyon Trail and climbs steeply for 0.8 of a mile. After a half mile, the Phoneline Trail cuts off to the right. This is a popular tram-hike loop for people who ride the tram up and hike the 4 miles back down the Phoneline Trail to lower Sabino Canyon.

After a few more switchbacks, the trail levels off along the top of the ridge. The city is now out of sight. To the left and far below is Sabino Creek. There are a few uphill, rocky spots, but for the most part, the trail is a gradual and easy climb as it meanders its way along the side of the ridge. After a mile and a half the trail makes a sharp curve to the right and begins descending quickly.

Follow the West Fork of Sabino Trail to the left for 1.6 miles until you reach the turnoff on the right to Hutch's Pool. Cairns mark the trail, which now follows the left, or west, side of the creek. After a quarter mile, several paths to the right lead down to the creek. The first side trail leads to a large pool, which is a lovely spot but is not the actual Hutch's Pool. Continue ahead. The trail now bears left away from the stream for 0.2 of a mile. When the trail begins to climb slightly, look for a cairn in front of a large oak tree. A trail leads to the right, down to the stream to Hutch's Pool, which is long and narrow, with cliffs on each side and a waterfall at the north end.

It takes two to three hours to reach Hutch's Pool, depending on how long you linger along the way. If you care to explore a little farther, there are other smaller pools a few hundred yards upstream.

THE
SANTA RITA
MOUNTAINS

For nearly three hundred years, mankind has sought the gold and silver in the Santa Rita Mountains. The Spanish were the first to look for the treasures.

The Spanish established a mission at Tumacacori and a presidio at Tubac, both in the shadow of the Santa Rita Mountains. Jesuit priests sent Indian labor to the mines in the Santa Rita Mountains in the 1700s. By the mid-1800s, Apache attacks had forced the abandonment of the mission, the presidio, and the attempts to mine.

When the area became part of the United States with the Gadsden Purchase, attempts were again made at ranching and mining. So rich was the Santa Cruz Valley and the Santa Rita Mountains, that they were the scene of constant battles over ownership. Huge Spanish land grants were supposedly to be honored by the Mexican government, and later, by the United States government. Complicating matters were the claims of the heirs of the Baca Float, who claimed the land as replacement for land they had once claimed in New Mexico. The disputes went all the way to the United States Supreme Court and are too complicated to discuss here.

Eventually the heirs of the Baca Float got much of the land in the Santa Cruz Valley, but not without vigorous attempts to claim a large area of the Santa Ritas. In pursuing their claims, two men were sent to survey the mountains. Both were killed by Apaches. Mount Wrightson and Mount Hopkins bear their names.

When most of the Apaches were confined to reservations, mining in the Santa Ritas boomed. Towns grew overnight. Greaterville had a population of 500 by 1879, a public school, a post office, and several saloons. Driving through what remains of the town en route to a hiking trail, it is hard to visualize that 500 people once lived there. On the north side of the Santa Ritas, the town of Helvetia boasted a population of 400 by 1891. Today all that remains are a few buildings and a cemetery.

Look at the map of the Santa Ritas. The canyons are dotted with the names of mines. Josephine Canyon, Gardner Canyon, and Temporal Gulch all once touted major mining operations. It did not last. By the early 1900s most of the mines had played out. Today Helvetia and Greaterville are ghost towns. The gold of the Santa Rita Mountains now lies in the hiking trails and beautiful backcountry of the mountains. The Santa Ritas were made part of the Coronado National Forest in 1908 and are now a National Wilderness Area.

As this edition goes to press, controversy continues about the development of the Rosemont Mine along Route 83 in the northern foothills of the Santa Rita Mountains. Supporters of the mine contend that it will provide much needed employment and bring billions of dollars into the local economy. Opponents say that the mine will take thousands of acres of the Coronado National Forest out of recreational use and decrease the quality of life of nearby residents.

The Santa Ritas.

Old Baldy Trail

General Description: A much-used trail to the summit of the highest peak in the Santa Rita Mountains, with spectacular views most of the way up and from the top

Difficulty: Difficult, some areas of exceptionally steep climbing

Best Time of Year to Hike: Spring, fall, summer

Length: 10.8 miles round-trip

Miles to Trailhead from Speedway/Campbell Intersection: 43.5 miles

Directions to Trailhead from Speedway/Campbell Intersection: Go west on Speedway until you reach the intersection of I-10. Follow I-10 to the intersection of I-19 (the Nogales Exit). Follow I-19 to Green Valley. From Green Valley, follow the brown signs to Madera Canyon, getting off at Exit 63. Continue following the signs to Madera Canyon, through Continental, to the upper end of the canyon. The Old Baldy Trail begins in the Mount Wrightson Picnic Area located at the end of Madera Canyon Road.

Fees: There is a fee to access Madera Canyon. The fee may be paid in cash or with one of the available passes. The yearly Coronado Recreation Pass ($20) may be purchased at the Santa Rita Lodge in upper Madera Canyon. Daily ($5) and weekly ($10) passes are available from fee boxes in the campgrounds. The America the Beautiful pass is also accepted in Madera Canyon.

■ ■ ■

One never knows exactly what to expect while hiking the popular Mount Wrightson trail. As I pulled into the parking lot at 7:00 A.M. one Sunday in early June, I was surprised to have difficulty finding a

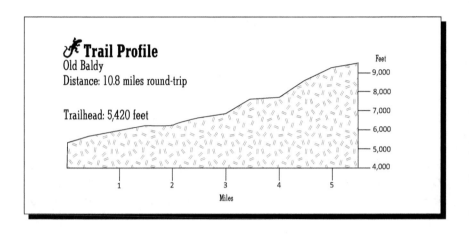

Trail Profile
Old Baldy
Distance: 10.8 miles round-trip

Trailhead: 5,420 feet

place to park. Then I discovered that a canopy had been set up, and a wedding was in progress. About a mile into the hike I was nearly scared witless by a moving brown object that I thought was a bear, but it was a man and his tripod, both completely covered with camouflage netting. Farther along the trail I met a backpacker with a full-sized guitar attached to his pack. At Bellows Spring I met a man celebrating his sixtieth birthday by taking his poodle, complete with neckerchief, to "sign in" on the summit of Wrightson. (He made it, and I photographed him at the top!) Near Baldy Saddle, I had to dodge a group of runners returning from the summit. One had made it to the top in one hour and thirty-six minutes. It would take me nearly five hours!

The Old Baldy Trail to the summit of Mount Wrightson is the most direct route to the 9,453-foot peak, the highest in the Santa Rita Mountain Range. It is also the steepest and most difficult route. The trail name refers to Old Baldy, the original name of Mount Wrightson. It was renamed in memory of William Wrightson, who was killed by Apaches in 1865 as he was attempting to survey this area to establish the claims of the Baca heirs. His assistant, Gilbert Hopkins, was killed at the same time, and nearby Mount Hopkins is named in his honor.

The trailhead is 0.3 of a mile up an old road that leaves from the south end of the parking area. The Old Baldy Trail makes a sharp left at a signed intersection. The signs in the Santa Rita Mountains are superior to many signed trails. Made of metal, with the trail name etched

Old Baldy Trail

0 ¹/₂ 1

1 mile

through the metal, and attached by pipes set in concrete, they are usually safe from destruction by man or beast!

The trail begins to climb immediately under a canopy of silverleaf oak trees. After about 200 yards there is a large, green water tank to the left. This is the holding tank for the water that supplies the homes and businesses in Madera Canyon.

This is a heavily used trail, and over the years, many persons have shortcut the trail. This unnecessary practice has caused erosion, and in several areas the trail has been rerouted. The old portion of the trail is often covered with dead limbs or otherwise blocked so that the correct route is always easy to follow.

The trail continues to gain elevation quickly. One of the best things about the Old Baldy Trail is the views. You can see Green Valley, the pecan orchards, and the copper mines to the northwest and, as you get higher, the telescopes atop Mount Hopkins to the southwest.

Most of the trail follows the north or east side of the ridge. There are several small drainages that cross the trail that may have water, depending on the time of year you are hiking. After about one mile, you cross a large side drainage and then wind around the east side of the hill to an open area that was once used as a helicopter landing pad. Past the open area, the trail reenters the forest, now consisting of oak and ponderosa pine.

After crossing two small drainages, the trail goes slightly downhill, across a large drainage, and climbs along the side of the mountain. In this section, the trail splits, and there is a rather distinct trail that goes to the left. The correct route is the wide trail straight ahead. There are several faint trails in this area that lead down to one of a number of secluded camp spots in the ravine. The trail continues along the west side of this ravine and is a lovely area.

Soon the trail begins to switchback steeply. This is one area that has been rerouted, but the main trail is always evident. The switchbacks become longer and end at Josephine Saddle. It will take about two hours to reach the saddle.

Josephine Saddle is a crossroads for several trails. The mysterious Josephine of the Santa Ritas has a saddle, a canyon, and a peak named in her honor. The saddle is a beautiful area, covered with tall ponderosa, Apache, Arizona white, and Chihuahua pines. It is a favorite camping area, and it is a rare hike when you do not see a tent set up under a tree.

There are a number of signs in the saddle. The Old Baldy Trail leaves the saddle to the east, past the cross marking the death of three Boy Scouts, who camped in the vicinity of the saddle on November 15, 1958, when an unusually severe winter storm hit Tucson. The cross and plaque were placed there by their Boy Scout troop. Wreaths and flowers are frequently placed on the cross, which serves not only as a memorial but as a reminder of the potential danger to those of us who hike and camp on this mountain. A new memorial has been placed at the beginning of the Super Trail to commemorate the fiftieth anniversary of the boys' deaths.

A few yards past the memorial, the Temporal Canyon Trail cuts off to the right. Follow the arrows to the left to Mount Wrightson. The trail

View of Mount Wrightson from the Old Baldy Trail.

to Baldy Saddle switchbacks gradually and, in this section, is sandy and smooth. After the second switchback, you can see the other side of the mountain, including the observatory on Mount Hopkins. The trail goes around the south side of the mountain and climbs gradually. After 0.8 of a mile, you come to a sign indicating the cutoff of the Super Trail to the right. You want to continue left on the Old Baldy Trail. From here Bellows Spring is 1.1 miles; Baldy Saddle, 1.8; and the summit, 2.7. The trail continues to gain elevation, and the views are excellent as it works its way up the mountain.

Soon the trail turns to the right sharply and switchbacks up the mountain. As the switchbacks get steeper, the views get better! There is a short, level area for about a quarter of a mile, with Mount Wrightson towering above you, before the switchbacks begin again in earnest. Finally the trail levels out in the vicinity of Bellows Spring. Clear, cold water pours into the tank and it is tempting, though unsafe, to take a drink.

Past the spring, the trail is very rocky and exceptionally pretty. It is a brushy trail, with a series of short, rocky switchbacks. A few hundred yards past the spring is a stand of young aspen, but, for the most part, the vegetation consists of thick shrubs. The views up this final section of the trail to Baldy Saddle are excellent. You are about eye level with Mount Hopkins, site of the Smithsonian Institute and University of Arizona's Fred A. Whipple Observatory. To the northwest you can see another famous observatory, Kitt Peak. Baboquivari, the sacred mountain of the Tohono O'Odham Tribe, is the bald, rounded summit southwest of Kitt Peak. From one vantage point, you may be able to spot your car in the Madera Canyon parking lot.

As the switchbacks approach the saddle, you can see that there has been much shortcutting in the past. Excellent trail reconstruction has been done to discourage the practice and to make the final few switchbacks very evident. The saddle itself is barren compared to Josephine Saddle. Still, the area is much used as a camping spot. Even on the hottest summer day in Tucson, the temperature in the 8,050-foot saddle is delightful.

From the saddle it is 0.9 of a mile to the summit of Mount Wrightson. The trail begins at the south end of the saddle and, for nearly half a mile, is gradual, along the side of the mountain. It goes through tall pines, and the trail is covered with pine needles, making it a welcome change. Of course, this cannot last, and the trail quickly becomes a series of rocky switchbacks with only one break to the top. This rocky, steep trail rounds to the south side of the mountain and climbs to the summit. An excellent interpretive sign explains that this summit was a fire lookout from the 1920s through the 1950s. The remains of the foundation are of a fire lookout cabin that was built in 1928.

The summit of Mount Wrightson has views that, on a clear day, are spectacular. Take a map with you and spend some time picking out the various mountain ranges and the cities that you can see from the top.

Only two things can mar the feeling of accomplishment that you have in climbing this summit. First, if you should be there in June, the ladybugs claim this summit as their own, as do millions of other small insects. Having been warned by hikers coming down from the top, I covered myself with insect repellent, and the bugs loved it! A second problem is the air pollution that too frequently obscures the view.

But on a clear day, standing atop Mount Wrightson, you can understand why people get married in its shadow and carry guitars and poodles to the top. However, it will always be hard for me to understand why anyone runs to the summit!

Super Trail

General Description: A practically painless way to climb to the summit of Mount Wrightson, this is a gradual trail with some especially beautiful sections

Difficulty: Difficult

Best Time of Year to Hike: Spring, fall, summer

Length: 16.4 miles round-trip

Miles to Trailhead from Speedway/Campbell Intersection: 43.5 miles

Directions to Trailhead from Speedway/Campbell Intersection: Go west on Speedway until you reach the intersection of I-10. Follow I-10 to the intersection of I-19 (the Nogales Exit). Follow I-19 to Green Valley. From Green Valley, follow the brown signs to Madera Canyon, getting off at Exit 63. Continue following the signs to Madera Canyon, through Continental, to the upper end of the canyon. A sign indicates parking for trails. The Super Trail begins in the Mount Wrightson Picnic Area located at the end of Madera Canyon Road.

Fees: There is a fee to access Madera Canyon. The fee may be paid in cash or with one of the available passes. The yearly Coronado Recreation Pass ($20) may be purchased at the Santa Rita Lodge in upper Madera Canyon. Daily ($5) and weekly ($10) passes are available from fee boxes in the campgrounds. The America the Beautiful pass is also accepted in Madera Canyon.

■ ■ ■

The Super Trail is the easiest, but longest, route to the summit of Mount Wrightson. It begins to the left of the Mount Wrightson Picnic Area at the end of the Madera Canyon Road.

The trail parallels the right side of the creek, which has water much of the year. There are nice camping spots beside the creek. The trail passes under tall oaks, juniper pines, and Arizona sycamores. After one-quarter of a mile the trail crosses the creek and heads to the left, in the first of several long, gradual switchbacks. As you turn on the second switchback, there are excellent views of your final goal—Mount Wrightson. The elevation gain is so gradual that almost without realizing it, you are high above the canyon.

The trail goes in and out of shady areas, with several varieties of oak and a few ponderosa pine providing shade. Several side ravines cross the trail. At certain times of year there would be water trickling down these ravines. Whatever the time of year, the drainages make very green, pretty areas, often with wildflowers growing. Mount Wrightson pops in and out of view as the trail once again begins to parallel the creek. The creek by now will have small pools in all but the driest of seasons.

After a half mile, the trail again leaves the creek and begins to switchback up the side of the canyon. As you gain in elevation, the views of the valley and the canyon are wider. Green Valley, the dark green of the pecan orchards, and the mines are visible. One long switchback heads north, away from Josephine Saddle, and comes to a point of the ridge. Here the views of the valley are especially impressive.

As the trail rounds the ridge and once again heads south toward Josephine Saddle, it reenters a shady area with ponderosa and Apache pines and a few spruce. The trail opens up briefly, and now you can see the observatory on top of Mount Hopkins. Also you can look down on the Old Baldy Trail headed to Josephine Saddle on the other side of the canyon.

Past the sign is another exceptionally lovely area. There are pines, oaks, and an occasional open area. Two-tenths of a mile before Josephine Saddle is Sprung Spring. A round metal tank with water piped in is a welcome sight. It is always running, and although it should be purified before drinking, it is nice to know that this permanent source of water is available. The trees surrounding the spring are tall,

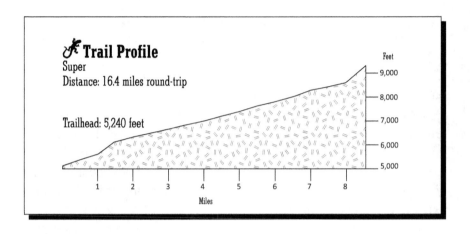

and the vegetation is lush. This is a great area for wildlife spotting, especially in early evening. A faint trail going downhill from the spring leads to the Little Shot Mine, should you be interested in a side exploration. The opening has been partially cemented for safety.

Past the spring the trail switchbacks quickly into Josephine Saddle, coming out right at the sign that marks the deaths of three Boy Scouts, who were camped in the vicinity of the saddle on November 15, 1958, when an unusually severe winter storm hit Tucson.

At this crossroads it is possible to leave the Super Trail and continue your ascent of Mount Wrightson by the Old Baldy Trail. This would shorten the hike considerably, but add greatly to the steepness. I'll assume that you plan to go all the way to Baldy Saddle via the Super Trail. To do this, turn left at the signed intersection, following the arrow to Mount Wrightson. The trail switchbacks to the left and then quickly to the right. Continue up this switchback for approximately 200 yards to another signed intersection. Follow the sign to the right to continue your climb to Mount Wrightson via the Super Trail. From this point it is another 4.2 miles to the summit. The ascent is so gradual that this is practically a painless way to attain Baldy Saddle. Unfortunately, there is no painless way to make it to the summit of Mount Wrightson!

The trail climbs in a series of long, easy switchbacks at first and crosses a rocky area. From all along this portion of the trail there are excellent views of Mount Hopkins. The observatory atop

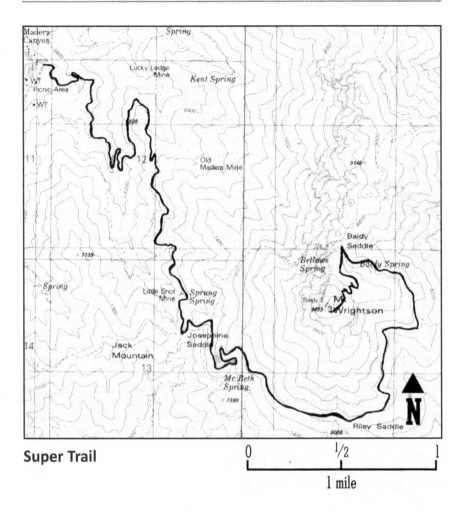

Super Trail

0   ¹/₂   1

1 mile

Mount Hopkins is a joint venture of the University of Arizona and the Smithsonian Institution.

As the trail winds around the mountain, there are a couple of spots where the trail crosses rock falls. For about a mile the trail goes through a grassy area with clumps of grass and a few pine and small oak. The basic plan of the trail is to go around the south side of Mount Wrightson. The trail continues to gradually work its way around the mountain, coming to the drainage that comes down from Mount Wrightson. Here are large rocks, a large alligator juniper, and a huge ponderosa pine.

Memorial on the Super Trail.

Farther up the drainage, you can see a stand of aspen. The trail leaves this drainage and continues through an open area to a trail intersection. The trail to the right leads off to Gardner Canyon. You should continue left and around Mount Wrightson.

Soon you leave the open area and come into a beautiful section of the trail. Several long switchbacks lead through tall ponderosas and Douglas fir trees to Baldy Saddle. Right before reaching Baldy Spring, there is an oft-used campsite with logs for sitting and the ever-present fire ring. Almost immediately past this campsite is Baldy Spring. The tank is nearly always full, and the water can be used if it is purified. In half a mile from the spring, you are at Baldy Saddle. The Super Trail ends at Baldy Saddle, and you turn left and join the Old Baldy Trail to the summit.

You can return from Mount Wrightson down the Super Trail, the Old Baldy Trail, or a combination of both. If the entire hike is done on the Super Trail, it is a total of 16.4 miles. That makes for a very long hike, regardless of how gradual it is. Hikers soon learn the combination that most suits their hiking style.

Kent Spring–Bog Springs Loop Trail

General Description: A loop trail past three springs through a riparian area

Difficulty: Moderate, some areas of steep climbing

Best Time of Year to Hike: Spring, fall, winter

Length: 5.4 mile loop

Miles to Trailhead from Speedway/Campbell Intersection: 42 miles

Directions to Trailhead from Speedway/Campbell Intersection: Go west on Speedway until you reach the intersection of I-10. Follow I-10 east to the intersection of I-19 (the Nogales Exit). Follow I-19 to Green Valley. Leave the freeway at Exit 63. Go left under I-19, following the signs to Madera Canyon, through Continental, to the Madera Trailhead parking area on your left soon after you enter the Canyon. The Kent Spring–Bog Springs Loop Trail begins at the lower end of the parking area.

Fees: There is a fee to access Madera Canyon. The fee may be paid in cash or with one of the available passes. The yearly Coronado Recreation Pass ($20) may be purchased at the Santa Rita Lodge in upper Madera Canyon. Daily ($5) and weekly ($10) passes are available from fee boxes in the campgrounds. The America the Beautiful pass is also accepted in Madera Canyon.

■ ■ ■

The Kent Spring–Bog Springs Loop is one of the prettiest hikes in the Santa Rita Mountains. A series of springs creates an unusually lush area that attracts a large number of birds and wildlife. Large Arizona walnut and sycamore trees provide a canopy that invites you to relax and spend the better part of a day before returning to the arid environment of southeastern Arizona.

Follow the trail sign at the lower end of the parking area to the beginning of the Kent Spring–Bog Springs Loop Trail. From this point it is approximately 0.4 mile to the beginning of the loop. You may go first to Bog Springs and then circle to Kent Spring and back to the trailhead, or reverse the direction. I prefer to hike to Bog Springs first, so the following directions will describe the loop in that direction.

To the north and northwest, the views of Kitt Peak, the copper mines, Green Valley, and surrounding communities stand out as you gain in elevation. After climbing steadily for nearly a mile, the trail drops into Bog Springs. There is a concrete tank and a spigot for water a short distance beyond the tank. *Webster's* defines bog as "wet, spongy ground." This area comes as close to that definition as is possible in southeastern Arizona. The reedlike horsetail grows in abundance. There are huge Arizona sycamores, many of them with hollowed-out trunks that would be large enough to shelter a person caught in a storm. Beyond the spring are two stone-covered tanks, and farther up the canyon, there are several small, concrete tanks. There are huge fir trees, Arizona walnut trees, and again many Arizona sycamores.

As the trail leaves the spring and climbs the side of the canyon, there is an almost total change in vegetation. What was a green and

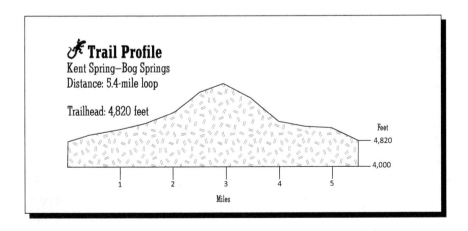

Trail Profile
Kent Spring–Bog Springs
Distance: 5.4-mile loop

Trailhead: 4,820 feet

Feet
4,820
4,000

1　2　3　4　5

Miles

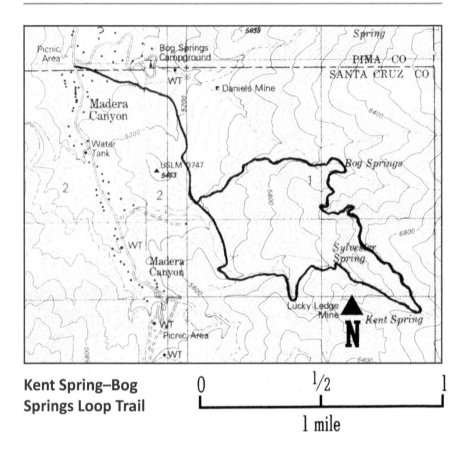

Kent Spring–Bog Springs Loop Trail

0 1/2 1

1 mile

lush canyon becomes a scrub-oak covered, dry ridge. The trail switchbacks as it climbs to Kent Spring and the beginning of the Kent Spring Trail. There are excellent views of Mount Wrightson. Past this point, a few more switchbacks, and you are on top of the ridge. A large log, worn smooth by many resting hikers, invites you to sit and take in the views. Now Baboquivari and Kitt Peaks are both visible.

Past the log, the trail is fairly level along the side of the ridge, with some moderate uphill. Several points in this area are rocky, and the shale covering the trail, in combination with the narrowness of the trail, makes it easy to fall. As the trail goes back into the forest, walking becomes easy again. As you approach Kent Spring, huge Arizona sycamores again dominate the scene. There is a small stream that runs

Hiker tests the water at Kent Spring.

most of the year. The area is not quite as green as Bog Springs, but it is very close. Across the stream is a round, stone tank that is Kent Spring.

This spring was most likely named for W. H. B. Kent, a supervisor in the Tumacacori Division of the Forest Service from 1904 until 1908. Kent was a maverick ranger, wearing a bandanna instead of the regulation Stetson, and holding meetings near a spring in the Santa Ritas, where he read poetry to his charges. His fondness for whiskey earned him the nickname "Whiskey High Balls" Kent. By 1911, Kent was "eased" out of the Forest Service and, after serving in France during World War I, he moved to California where he wrote Western novels. His *The Tenderfoot* and *Range Rider* were published by New York's Macmillan and Company. Copies may be found at the University of Arizona Library, Special Collections section.

At the spring, the trail goes sharply right and becomes a jeep road. It is all downhill from here, except for a few short portions near the end. The road follows the stream down the mountain and is lovely. After about a half mile, you come to Sylvester Spring, which consists of a large concrete tank and two smaller tanks. This spring probably bears the name of Art and Anna Sylvester, who had a summer cabin in Madera Canyon in the 1930s.

Past the spring, the road is uphill for a very short time and is no longer rocky. For much of the way the road follows the left bank of the stream. At a pipeline, the trail crosses the stream and, depending on the time of year, can require wading. This entire portion along the stream is beautiful, with tall trees and, hopefully, the sound of water running. You often see deer along this stream.

As the trail approaches the end, it becomes sandy, as it pulls away from the stream and out into the open. Look carefully for the turnoff to the left to return to the parking area.

Dutch John Spring Trail

General Description: A short, pleasant hike, through an evergreen oak forest to Dutch John Spring and beyond

Difficulty: Moderate

Best Time of Year to Hike: Spring, fall, winter

Length: 3.6 miles round-trip

Miles to Trailhead from Speedway/Campbell Intersection: 44 miles

Directions to Trailhead from Speedway/Campbell Intersection: Drive west on Speedway to I-10. Turn left under I-10. Follow I-10 until you reach the intersection of I-19 (Nogales Exit). Follow I-19 through Green Valley to Exit 63. At Exit 63 go left under I-19, following the signs to Madera Canyon. Turn left at the sign indicating the Bog Springs Campground and drive to the top where the restrooms are located. There are six parking places for hikers by the restrooms in the Bog Springs Campground. Follow trail signs directly across from the restrooms to the beginning of the Dutch John Spring Trail.

Fees: There is a fee to access Madera Canyon. The fee may be paid in cash or with one of the available passes. The yearly Coronado Recreation Pass ($20) may be purchased at the Santa Rita Lodge in upper Madera Canyon. Daily ($5) and weekly ($10) passes are available from fee boxes in the campgrounds. The America the Beautiful pass is also accepted in Madera Canyon.

■ ■ ■

The Santa Rita Mountains hold many mysteries. One involves "Dutch John." Surely someone didn't just find this spring and say, "Why don't we name this Dutch John Spring?" There must be more to the story.

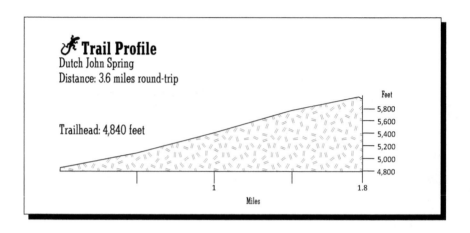

A search of the Santa Cruz County Courthouse records and the Pimeria Alta Historical Society library in Nogales turned up a John Tannenbaum, a man of German descent, born in the German section of Fredericksburg, Texas, who moved to the Patagonia area after, some say, having killed a man in Texas.

Tannenbaum worked on ranches in the Santa Ritas and was known locally as "the Dutchman." In 1926, while working as a cook for the 7V Ranch roundup, Tannenbaum killed a man who told him to bridle his horse. According to Frank Seibold's *Tales From Sonoita*, Tannenbaum told the man he "did not do bridles." A heated argument followed and the man never made another such request (or any other request for that matter). Nothing links John Tannenbaum to Dutch John Spring, but it makes a good story!

The hike to the spring begins directly across from the restrooms where a large map shows the trails in the area. A few steps lead to a small sign that indicates the beginning of the Dutch John Trail.

After you've been on the trail a few feet look to your left for the grave of Sopy, a pet whose lifespan lasted from 1996 to 1998. The trail begins to climb, passing two very large water tanks on the right. Immediately past the water tanks is a fence and a "people only" pass-through metal gate. The trail is at first a gradual climb, with the creek on the right. The canyon is filled with Arizona sycamore and several varieties of oak trees. Evergreen oaks—silverleaf, Arizona white, and

The "first" Dutch John Spring.

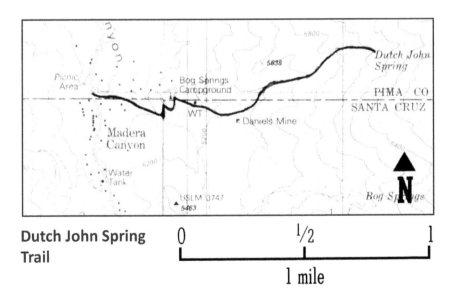

Dutch John Spring Trail

Emory—are a trademark of this trail and grow unusually large because of the abundance of water here.

A sign marks the wilderness boundary, as you pass under a canopy of the beautiful oaks. Past the boundary marker, the trail gets steeper, and the leaves on the trail make it slippery. These evergreen oaks do lose their leaves, but unlike the deciduous Gambel oak, new leaves immediately replace old ones, thus the term live oaks.

In about 0.6 of a mile after leaving the campground, a path leads to the left, to what is marked with a metal sign that says, "Dutch John Spring." A small bathtub-shaped tank provides water for wildlife. It is a pleasant area with large Arizona sycamores interspersed with oaks and junipers.

This trail is too beautiful to stop at Dutch John Spring. Past the spring the trail gets steeper. A few pine trees begin to appear, indicating that you are entering a higher elevation. The trail ends at a rocky area where water tumbles down the mountain and brightly colored flowers dot the landscape. Sit down and rest awhile. Listen to rippling water and watch as hummingbirds dart about. You've earned it!

Agua Caliente (Vault Mine)– Josephine Saddle Loop Trail

General Description: A little-used trail past an old mine that provides out-standing views

Difficulty: Difficult, some areas of exceptionally steep climbing

Best Time of Year to Hike: Spring, fall, summer

Length: 6.5 miles—Old Baldy return; 7.4 miles—Super Trail return

Miles to Trailhead from Speedway/Campbell Intersection: 43.5 miles

Directions to Trailhead from Speedway/Campbell Intersection: Go west on Speedway until you reach the intersection of I-10. Follow I-10 to the intersection of I-19 (the Nogales Exit). Remain on I-19 until you reach Green Valley. Follow the brown signs to Madera Canyon, getting off at Exit 63. Follow the signs to Madera Canyon. Drive to the upper part of Madera Canyon to the Mount Wrightson Picnic Area where signs indicate parking for trails. Pick up a "Hiking in Madera Canyon" trail map at the trailhead sign.

Fees: There is a fee to access Madera Canyon. The fee may be paid in cash or with one of the available passes. The yearly Coronado Recreation Pass ($20) may be purchased at the Santa Rita Lodge in upper Madera Canyon. Daily ($5) and weekly ($10) passes are available from fee boxes in the camp-grounds. The America the Beautiful pass is also accepted in Madera Canyon.

■ ■ ■

The Vault Mine portion of this hike is VERY STEEP, gaining 1,400 vertical feet in 1.5 miles. Don't dismay! When you come to the intersection of the Agua Caliente Trail, it's mostly level and downhill back to the parking lot. As a loop trail through Josephine Saddle, it is one of the prettiest hikes in Madera Canyon.

The Vault Mine Trail begins 0.3 of a mile up the old road that leads south from the parking area. At 0.3 of a mile, you come to the first trail intersection. To the left is the Old Baldy Trail to Josephine Saddle. Turn right following the sign to Agua Caliente Trail, the one indicated on the sign as being a "Very Steep Trail." The old road parallels Madera Creek. Usually there is some water flowing in the stream. Tall Arizona sycamores and several varieties of oak shade the area. More than two hundred species of birds have been spotted in Madera Canyon, including the rare, colorful elegant trogon. The last time I hiked this trail, I saw two elegant trogons.

As the road steepens, keep looking for a side trail on the right that crosses the stream. This area is used heavily, and there are many side trails leading down to the stream. The correct trail crosses Madera Creek and passes to the right of a large silverleaf oak tree. In about 200 yards, a sign indicates that the Agua Caliente Trail is to the right by way of the Vault Mine Trail. From here, it is 3.7 miles to Josephine Saddle.

Past the sign, the trail soon follows a ledge far above Madera Creek.

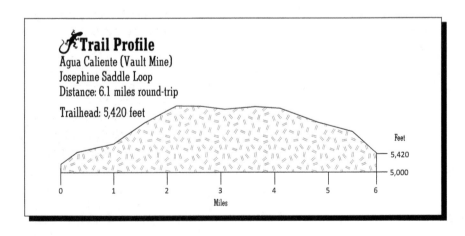

⚞Trail Profile
Agua Caliente (Vault Mine)
Josephine Saddle Loop
Distance: 6.1 miles round-trip

Trailhead: 5,420 feet

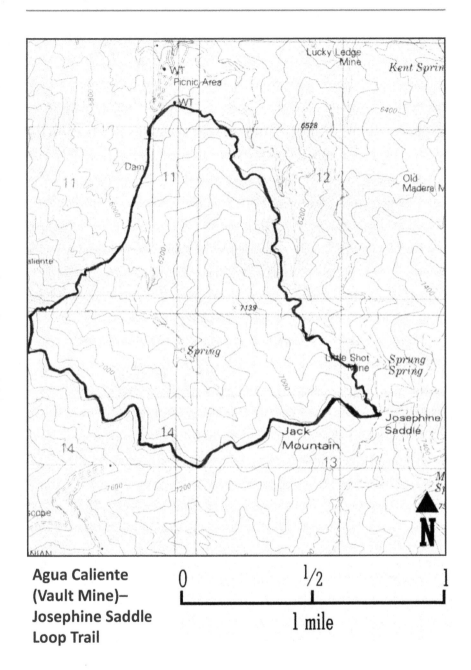

Agua Caliente (Vault Mine)– Josephine Saddle Loop Trail

0   1/2   1

1 mile

Hiker standing by the Lead Prospect Mine.

This is a beautiful area, with large oaks and pines. It is level only briefly, before beginning a series of steep switchbacks. After the first set of switchbacks, the trail comes to an open area, and you can see the Santa Catalina Mountains and part of Tucson, before the trail again switchbacks up the mountain.

As the trail rounds to the east side of the mountain, it opens up, and the trees are not as thick. It is again very rocky and steep. After 0.6 of a mile and a 1,400-foot-elevation gain, you come to an abandoned mine tunnel.

This is not the Treasure Vault Mine, as the trail name would suggest, but the Lead Prospect Mine. The Treasure Vault Mine is on the other side of the saddle and can be reached by continuing on the Agua Caliente Trail. Mining in this area dates to the arrival of the Jesuit fathers in the 1680s, who used Indian labor to search for gold and silver. However, by the time of the Gadsden Purchase in 1854, when this area became part of the United States, Apache raids made mining too dangerous. It was not until after the Civil War that American miners once again entered the area.

The trail beyond the mine, with the exception of the first 200 yards, is exceptionally steep and rocky. At 1.2 miles you come to a signed intersection. Turn left to Josephine Saddle. Now the steep part of the trail is over, as it circles the mostly open, northeast side of the mountain. Although there are a few steep drop-offs and several areas where the trail crosses rockfalls, the trail is a joy to hike from here to Josephine Saddle.

During the first part of this section of trail, there are some very large oak trees. The last time I hiked this trail there were hundreds of small pine trees along the trail, so thick that in several places I found myself putting my foot down, hoping that there was not a rattler in there shading itself! The trail goes in and out of cover, under huge box elder and pine trees. In spring, the pink blossoms of locust trees lend a pleasant fragrance to the air. There is also a section of large, beautiful aspen, one of the few areas of aspen in the Santa Ritas.

Past this lookout point, the trail goes downhill gradually and comes to a short saddle, before once again gaining in elevation. There is an open area covered with ferns that looks like it was once a burn area. Past this burn area, the trail reenters the woods and goes downhill gradually until it reaches Josephine Saddle.

As you will see, Josephine Saddle is a crossroads for many trails, which makes it possible to come up with any number of loops. For this particular loop, you may return to the parking area via the Old Baldy Trail (page 177, 2.2 miles) or the Super Trail (page 184, 3.7 miles). The choice depends on the condition of your legs and the amount of time you have allotted for hiking.

Elephant Head Trail

General Description: A difficult hike which begins on a trail, connects to an old mining road, and continues on a relatively new trail to the top of a massive rock formation that resembles the head of an elephant when viewed from certain angles

Difficulty: Extremely difficult

Best Time of Year to Hike: Late fall, winter, early spring

Length: 8 miles round-trip

Miles to Trailhead from Speedway/Campbell Intersection: 46.4 miles

Directions to Trailhead from Speedway/Campbell Intersection: Follow Speedway west to Interstate 10. Follow I-10 east to Exit 260, the junction of Interstate 19 toward Green Valley. Drive south on I-19 to Canoa Road, Exit 56. Go around the roundabout and turn left under I-19. After going under I-19 , turn right on the Frontage Road and go 3 miles to Elephant Head Road. Turn left on Elephant Head Road. After you cross the Santa Cruz River and the railroad tracks, watch for Mt. Hopkins Road on the right. Turn right on Mt. Hopkins Road and go 5.5 miles to Forest Service Road 183. A sign indicates that this is the route to Agua Caliente Canyon and the KMSB radio towers. Turn left on FSR 183 for 2.5 miles. A high clearance vehicle is best on this part of the road but if you go slowly a passenger car can make it. The parking area is on the right just before the road makes a left turn, crosses Agua Caliente Wash, and starts climbing to the KMSB radio towers. The trail begins a few yards back down the road on the right and is signed as Trail 930.

■　■　■

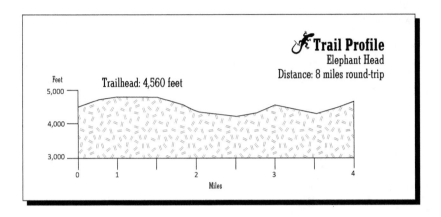

The 1887 Rand McNally map called this peak Picacho de Diablo or "Devil's Peak." Settlers in the Santa Cruz Valley believed that the Apache Indians used the peak as a lookout. There are stories that the Apaches took their enemies to the summit and tossed them to their death. I've been unable to determine how the name Elephant Head originated except that from certain angles, the massive rock outcropping looks like the head of an elephant.

Having hiked to the top of Elephant Head many times over the past twenty-five years, I can now say that my last trek to the summit in the spring of 2011 was the easiest yet. It's not that the elevation gain was less or that the route was less challenging. It's still a tough climb. The difference was that there is now a definitive trail leading across the last canyon to the summit.

My friend Chris and I left Tucson at 6:30 A.M. and were at the parking area a little before 8:00 A.M. The trail begins a few feet back down the road. Look on the right for a sign that says "Trail 930." The trail follows along a creek and is pleasant walking before beginning to climb. After nearly a mile of moderate climbing you reach a saddle that looks down into Chino Canyon, so named because Chinese workers built the road we were about to climb in the early 1900s. The Chinese also worked in the mines in the area. Descend into Chino Canyon and follow the sign that reads Quantrell Mine and points to the right.

Walk a short distance across the canyon and begin hiking up the well-constructed road that climbs steeply up the side of the mountain.

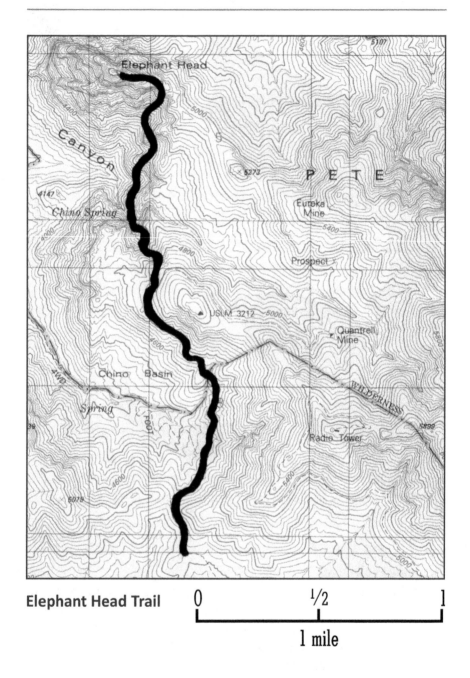

Elephant Head Trail

Just before you begin the climb, watch for a mine shaft on the right that is fenced off in a clear area of the road. While this is not the Quantrell Mine, it is one of many mines in the area. A skull and crossbones sign warns hikers not to enter the mine.

When you reach the top of the road you get a closer view of Elephant Head, which is now only one canyon away. Here you have the option to continue to the right for a little over a half mile along the road to the Quantrell Mine. This mine was located by Ben Daniels and two partners in 1907. Daniels, a Rough Rider in the Spanish-American War, was a close friend of Theodore Roosevelt. By 1912 the indicated values of the ore—which consisted of lead and zinc with traces of gold, silver, and copper—was valued from $12 to $15.85 per ton. You may choose to continue to the Quantrell Mine before beginning the climb of Elephant Head, but I suggest that you consider this option after returning from your ascent of Elephant Head.

Look for the trail that heads directly downhill and toward Elephant Head. It is marked by a large cairn. This trail goes steeply down to the creek and just as steeply up to the ridge that will take you

Elephant shrine on top of Elephant Head.

to the summit of Elephant Head. While looking for the trail, take a look at Elephant Head. It's getting more impressive!

The trail drops steeply down to the creek in the bottom of the canyon. This is the new part of the trail. The last time I hiked into this canyon, I had to bushwhack between the road and the saddle that leads to the top of Elephant Head. Most of the year there will be a pool at the bottom of the canyon. When you reach this spot, rest awhile before starting the difficult climb to the top of the ridge.

When you reach the top of the ridge, the trail turns to the left and goes up and down over some small outcroppings until you finally get to the saddle at the base of Elephant Head. Look around the area at the base of the massive rock formation and you will find pot shards indicating that prehistoric people lived or camped in this level spot.

After a brief rest, it's time to begin the final climb to the summit. Leave your hiking poles behind. They'll just be in the way. Look carefully for cairns that mark the route. Proceed slowly. Pause often to rest. At times it will seem unlikely that you can reach the top without ropes, but keep looking for cairns and remain calm. Soon you will see another route to climb to the next level. At one point we nearly gave up as we were having trouble finding foot and hand holds, but we rested a few minutes and helped each other to find foot and hand placements and were able to get to the top!

The views from the top are spectacular. Look to the South for an excellent view of Little Elephant Head, the flat-topped mountain we passed on the way up. To the East are Mount Hopkins and Mount Wrightson. Baboquivari, sacred mountain of the Tohono O'odham Nation, is clearly visible to the West.

Over the past several years, hikers have been carrying ceramic elephants to the top, creating an Elephant Shrine. There are at least fifty elephants of all designs and sizes piled on top of Elephant Head. Chris and I added our elephants to the shrine.

After adding our names to the sign-in book and eating our lunch, we began our descent. Need I say that the climb down Elephant Head was more difficult than the climb up? Or that when we reached the road leading to the Quantrell Mine, we decided to save that hike for another day even though it was only about another half mile to the mine? Will we ever hike to Elephant Head again? Yes!

Arizona Trail:
From Kentucky Camp to
Gardner Canyon Road

General Description: A hike along the Arizona Trail through a historic mining camp

Difficulty: Moderate

Best Time of Year to Hike: Fall, Winter, Spring

Length: 4.2 miles one way

Miles to Trailhead from Speedway/Campbell Intersection: 52 miles

Directions to Trailhead from Speedway/Campbell Intersection: Go west on Speedway Boulevard to Interstate 10. Get on I-10, heading east. Drive to Exit 281, State Highway 83 to Sonoita. Follow SH 83 for 21 miles to Gardner Canyon Road, which is on the right. Follow the signs to Kentucky Camp. The road from Gardner Canyon Road to the Kentucky Camp parking area is unpaved, but well graded and suitable for passenger cars. The total driving distance from Gardner Canyon Road to Kentucky Camp is 5.8 miles. Note: For this hike, it is convenient to take two vehicles. To do this, continue straight on Gardner Canyon Road for nearly 3 miles. Just past Apache Springs Ranch (on the left) is a large trailhead parking area on the right. Leave one vehicle here and drive to Kentucky Camp to begin the hike.

■ ■ ■

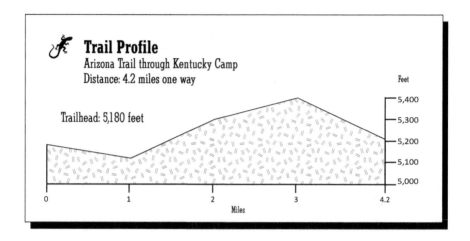

Trail Profile
Arizona Trail through Kentucky Camp
Distance: 4.2 miles one way

Trailhead: 5,180 feet

The Arizona Trail traverses the length of Arizona beginning at the Utah border, crossing the Grand Canyon, and ending at the Mexican border. The section of the trail from Kentucky Camp to Gardner Canyon Road is one of the most historic and scenic sections of the trail.

When you tell friends you are going to Kentucky Camp, they invariably ask, "Is that near Louisville?" No, Kentucky Camp (and Gulch) is right here in Arizona, probably named by or after a man from Kentucky who prospected here in the 1870s.

In 1903 James Stetson, a California mining engineer, convinced George B. McAneny of the famous Comstock Lode in Nevada, to join him in mining the area around Kentucky Camp. The two men formed the Santa Rita Water and Mining Company and built the adobe buildings that make up Kentucky Camp as company headquarters. Stetson designed an eight-mile ditch-pipeline system to deliver water to the mining site. Half of today's hike follows the route of this ditch.

The project was well underway when, on May 20, 1905, Stetson died in a fall from the third floor of the Santa Rita Hotel in Tucson. Shortly thereafter McAneny's wife sued him for divorce, tying up his funds. The company floundered and by 1908 ownership of the land, plus water and mineral rights, were held by Tucson businessman Louis Hummel. Hummel's daughter Flossie, and her husband, Wert Fenter, used the camp as a cattle ranch until the 1960s. Today Kentucky Camp is part of the Coronado National Forest.

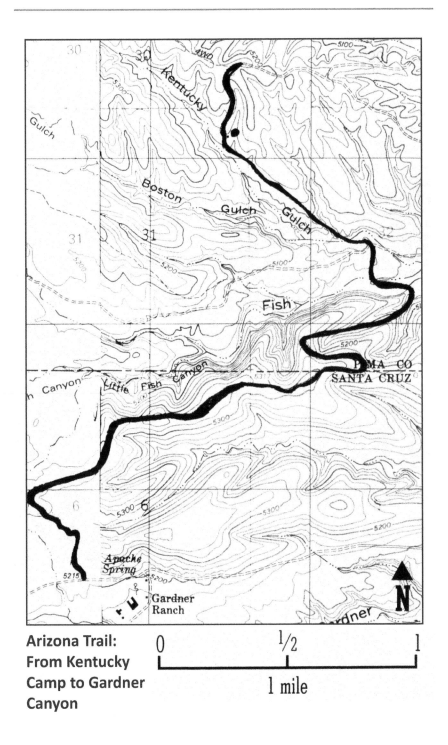

**Arizona Trail:
From Kentucky
Camp to Gardner
Canyon**

0   1/2   1

1 mile

Hiker pauses to look at the Administration Building
at Kentucky Camp.

After leaving a vehicle at the Gardner Canyon Road Trailhead, drive to the parking area for Kentucky Camp. From the parking area, walk down the road to Kentucky Camp.

Take time to explore the camp, starting with the administration building on the left. The visitor's room contains historic artifacts, photographs of volunteers restoring the site, a poster depicting a hike of the entire ditch, and brochures about the Friends of Kentucky Camp and rental of the Bed and No Breakfast.

After looking at the rest of the buildings, follow signs to the Arizona Trail. As you go through the gate, a trail to the right leads to Boston (a prospector from Boston?) Gulch, site of much of the mining in the area. Your route is to continue straight ahead on the Arizona Trail. Interpretive signs where Kentucky Gulch and Boston Gulch meet explains the process used to separate gold from lighter weight sands and gravels.

The trail leaves Boston Gulch and crosses Forest Road 4085, before climbing up a small hill. Through the gate the trail goes through a wooded area before climbing steeply to Forest Road 4180. Turn right, following signs for the Arizona Trail.

For over a mile the trail follows the road. The views in all directions are fit for a John Wayne movie. You are surrounded by mountain ranges. To the southwest is the highest peak in the Santa Rita Mountains, Mount Wrightson. In winter the 9,453-foot Wrightson is usually snowcapped. Due north are the Rincon Mountains. To the northeast are the Mustang, Whetstone, and Huachuca Mountains. Far in the distance to the north are the Santa Catalinas.

When the trail dips down and then climbs briefly near the end of the ridge, turn right for fifty yards to look at the penstock. This is the end of the ditch that begins at Bear Creek at the base of the Santa Rita Mountains. Water flowed into the penstock and was strained through screens to remove gravel and debris. The water was then compressed into high pressure hoses to use in hydraulic mining in Boston Gulch.

When you return to the trail, go straight, following the route of the ditch. This ditch was an ingenious system, alternating from the ditch to a pipeline and occasionally to a creek bed. It worked on the principle that as long as the beginning point of the water flow was higher than the end of the flow and never went higher than the starting point, it would reach its destination.

For the remainder of this section of the Arizona Trail note the changes from the open ditch to a pipeline. There are areas where the pipeline is exposed. At times the pipeline is covered by rocks for protection.

When you come to the head of the hill looking down on Gardner Canyon Road, note that the pipeline came up the steep embankment. If you have a vehicle waiting, climb down the ridge. If not, turn around and go back to Kentucky Camp.

Tunnel Spring Loop Trail

General Description: A loop hike from Tunnel Spring that climbs into the heart of the Santa Rita Mountains on Forest Service Road 785, the Cave Canyon–Gardner Canyon Cutoff segment, the Walker Basin Trail, and the Ditch

Difficulty: Difficult

Best Time of Year to Hike: Winter, early spring, late fall

Length: 10.3-mile loop

Miles to Trailhead from Speedway/Campbell Intersection: 56.6 miles

Directions to Trailhead from Speedway/Campbell Intersection: Go west on Speedway Boulevard to I-10. Continue east on I-10 for 20 miles until Exit 281. Drive south on Highway 83 for 21.5 miles to the signed exit to Kentucky Camp, which is on the right. You are now on FSR 92, also known as Gardner Canyon Road. Continue straight ahead on FSR 92 for 6.3 miles to a large signed parking area on the right just past Apache Springs Ranch. Past the parking area, watch carefully for a turnoff to the left on FSR 785. The turnoff is about one-half mile past the parking area. There is no mention of Tunnel Spring in the directional signs. Continue on FSR 785 for 3 miles to Tunnel Spring. The portion of the route past the turnoff requires a 4-wheel drive vehicle and cautious driving. Open the fenced gate for parking. This is the beginning of the Tunnel Spring Loop.

■　■　■

Whenever I can come up with a loop hike, I do it! Loop hikes have definite advantages. They start and end at the same place and only require one vehicle. Plus you see more scenery in the same

215

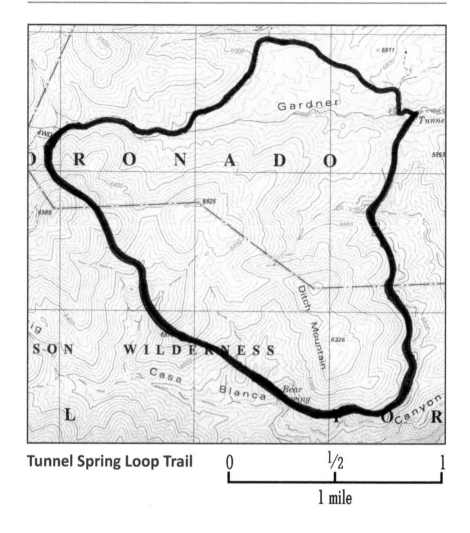

Tunnel Spring Loop Trail

0	¹/₂	1

1 mile

amount of hiking than you do with the typical out and back hike. So, read this description, get a map of the Santa Rita Mountains, and head for Tunnel Spring, the beginning and end of the Tunnel Spring Loop.

From Tunnel Spring, follow the road uphill for about a mile until you come to the Cave Canyon – Gardner Canyon cutoff to the left. As you climb you will soon begin to enjoy sweeping views of the surrounding area. Mount Wrightson looms high above you.

The Cave Canyon – Gardner Canyon segment of the loop climbs gradually to the end of the section. Much of the area has recovered from

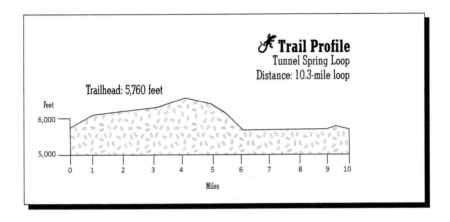

an extensive fire in the summer of 2005 although there are still a few sections of burned trees. When you reach the trailhead of the Walker Basin Trail, you will be at 6,480 feet. Turn left at the Walker Basin Trailhead sign where you will gain another 400 feet in elevation before heading downhill to Bear Spring, at 5,800 feet in elevation.

Walker Basin looms large in the history of Santa Rita Mountains. In 1883 Charles and Billy Owen came to the basin to start a cattle business. On April 27, 1886, Charlie, as he was known, was riding with a neighbor, A. L. Peck, when a band of Apaches attacked. Charlie was killed instantly. Peck's horse was shot from underneath him and he was captured by the Indians. They took his boots and warned him not to return to the ranch. Peck ignored the warning and walked barefoot to the ranch where he found his wife and baby slaughtered. Billy Owen went to California and asked his brother-in-law, William H. Walker, to come help him run the cattle business.

Walker sold his drugstore in California and arrived in the Arizona Territory with his wife, young son, and $250 dollars in cash, a substantial sum when cattle sold for $5 a head with a nursing calf thrown in for good measure. Walker's wife secured a teaching position at Calabasas and rode twelve miles from the ranch everyday to the school. Once, during an Indian scare, she spent the night in a walnut tree, afraid to continue on home. The Walkers remained in what became known as Walker Basin until 1921.

View from the Ditch section of the Tunnel Spring Loop Trail.

The hike down the Walker Basin Trail to Bear Spring is pleasant. This area did not suffer any fire damage and the trail is shaded by tall trees. As the trail levels out, look carefully on the left for a sign indicating the location of Bear Spring. The sign is confusing because it is not beside the spring. Continue to bear left and slightly downhill, until, except in long periods of drought, you hear the sounds of trickling water in Big Casa Blanca Canyon. While this is a beautiful spot to rest, don't linger too long—it's five miles along the Ditch back to Tunnel Spring.

The Ditch is part of the history of this area. In 1903 a California mining engineer, James Stetson, conceived a plan to provide a reliable water source for mining near Kentucky Camp. With capital from George McAneny of the famous Comstock Lode in Nevada, a ditch designed by Stetson was constructed from the creek in Big Casa Blanca Canyon to Tunnel Spring.

The system worked but was short-lived partly because of Stetson's untimely death on May 20, 1905, when he fell from a third-floor window of the Santa Rita Hotel in Tucson. Authorities never determined whether Stetson fell, jumped, or was pushed. McAneny could not save the mining operation because of marital difficulties resulting in a divorce that left him without enough money to operate Kentucky Camp.

Hiking the Ditch, which is a section of the Arizona Trail, is a good way to end this loop. You've already hiked almost seven miles and the Ditch is nearly level. Take time to notice the construction of the Ditch. The seven gates had moveable wooden slats that could be used in times of heavy runoff to release water and prevent erosion of the Ditch. Stetson insisted that these gates be made of California redwood, believing them to be more insect resistant than any Arizona wood. Remains of these slats can still be seen by some of the gates. Don't spend too much time looking down on the ground for slats and miss the views which, especially later in the day when the sun is sinking, are Western movie scenes.

The Ditch is flat until the end when the trail climbs up a short hill and down to Tunnel Spring. The water that flowed in the Ditch was directed through a tunnel and into the creek in Gardner Canyon where it connected with a series of pipelines and more ditches until it reached the top of a ridge above the mines near Kentucky Camp. To see the rest of the water system and visit Kentucky Camp, hike the Arizona Trail—From Kentucky Camp to Gardner Canyon (page 209).

SELECTED READINGS

Alexander, Kathy. *Paradise Found: The Settlement of the Santa Catalina Mountains.* Mount Lemmon, Ariz.: Skunkworks Productions, 1991. An excellent account of the "people history" of the Santa Catalina Mountains.

Bowden, Charles. *Frog Mountain Blues.* Tucson: The University of Arizona Press, 1987. The Tohono O'odham Indians call the Santa Catalinas "Frog Mountain." In this essay the author warns that this unique wilderness can be lost if it becomes too available to man.

Bowers, Janice. *The Mountains Next Door.* Tucson: The University of Arizona Press, 1991. Bowers writes beautifully of the Rincon Mountains, Tucson's last wilderness.

Burgess, Tony L., and Martha Ames Burgess. "Clouds, Spires and Spines," in *Tucson.* Tucson: Southwestern Mission Research Center, 1986. An essay about the past, present, and future of the Tucson area.

Gustafson, A. M., ed. *John Spring's Arizona.* Tucson: The University of Arizona Press, 1966. A series of articles written by John Spring, a teacher and soldier in the Arizona Territory in the 1870s.

Hanson, Roseann Beggy and Jonathan. *Southern Arizona Nature Almanac: A Seasonal Guide to Pima County and Beyond.* Boulder: Pruett Publishing Company, 1996.

Hufault, Cathy. *Death Clouds on Mt. Baldy: Tucson's Lost Tragedy.* Tucson: Arizona Mountain Publications, LLC, 2010.

Nabhan, Gary Paul. *Saguaro: A View of Saguaro National Monument and the Tucson Basin.* Tucson: Southwest Parks and Monuments Association, 1986. A collection of essays about the Saguaro National Monument with particular emphasis on the Rincon Mountain Unit.

Olin, George. *House in the Sun.* Tucson: Southwest Parks and Monuments Association, 1977. A complete narrative about the plants and animals living in the Sonoran Desert as well as an explanation of the desert environment.

Sonnichsen, C. L. *Tucson, the Life and Times of an American City.* Norman: The University of Oklahoma Press, 1982. Sonnichsen's folksy writing makes the history of Tucson seem like a novel.

ABOUT THE AUTHOR

Betty Leavengood enjoys keeping the *Tucson Hiking Guide*, which was first published in 1991, up-to-date by re-hiking the trails. "I'm always trying to figure out how to answer the question I get at book signings— 'Which trail is your favorite?' " she says. "I just can't decide!"

Photo by Jim Bowen

INDEX

Acropolis Cliffs, 122
Africanized bees, 11–12
Agua Caliente (Vault Mine)–Josephine
    Saddle Loop Trail, 199–203
Agua Caliente Hill Trail, 103–7
amole, 82, 138, 156
"A" Mountain (Sentinel Peak), 15–16,
    135, 148
Apaches, 15, 31, 65, 82, 101, 175, 178,
    202, 205, 217
Apache Spring, 156
Aravaipa Apache Nation, 31
Arizona Daily Star, 6, 37, 47, 54, 146
Arizona-Sonora Desert Museum, 17
Arizona Trail
    Hirabashi Recreation Site to Sabino
        Canyon, 165
    Kentucky Camp to Gardner Canyon
        Road, 209–14
    Quilter Trail, 67, 96, 99
    Rincon Peak Trail, 91
Aspen Fire, 102, 111
Ayres, James, 103

Baboquivari Peak, 104, 135, 144, 148,
    192
Baca Float, 175
Bain, Peter, 103
bajada, 21
Baldy Saddle, 178
Baldy Spring, 189
bark scorpions, 9
Bates, Stanford, 165
Bayers, Jon, 114
Bear Canyon Trail, 169

Bear Canyon Tram, 120, 122
Bear Creek, 213
bear grass, 82
Bear Spring, 218
bedrock mortars, 133, 150
bees, Africanized bees, 11–12
Bellows Spring, 178, 182
Big Casa Blanca Canyon, 218
Bingham, Tom, 148
Biosphere II, 134, 146, 152
Bird Canyon, 127
Blackett, Hill, Jr., 119–20
Blackett's Ridge Trail, 119–23
Bog Springs, Kent Spring–Bog Springs
    Loop Trail, 190–94
boots, 8
Boston Gulch, 213
Bowen House, 53, 54
Bowen, Jim, 113, 115, 118
Bowen, Pat, 114, 115, 118
Bowen, Sherry and Ruby, 54
Box Camp Canyon, 156
Box Camp Trail, 102, 153–58
Box Canyon, 65
Boy Scouts, 180, 188
Bridal Veil Falls, 128, 129
Bridal Wreath Falls, 88
Broadway Trailhead
Broadway Trailhead to Garwood Dam,
    73–77
    and Cactus Forest Trail, 70, 72
Brown, C. B., 16, 55
Brown Mountain Trail, 55–59
Bug Spring Trail, 108–12

Cactus Forest Trail, 68–72
Cactus Picnic Area, 125
cactus wren, 33
Cactus Wren Trail, 33
Cam-Boh Trail
Cam-Boh-Ironwood Forest–Picture
    Rocks Wash–Ringtail Loop, 60–64
    Roadrunner–Panther Peak Wash
    Cam-Boh Trail Loop, 45, 47, 49
Camp Lowell, 103
Canada del Oro Wash, 160
canteens, 5
Canyon Loop Trail, 160
Carlos III, King, 15
Carpenter, Dora, 137
Carpenter, Miles, 136–37
Carrillo, Emilio, 65
carrillo, Roger, 83
Carrillo Trail, 77
Catalina Forest Preserve, 102
Catalina Game Preserve, 146
Catalina Highway, 102, 111
Catalina State Park, Mount Lemmon to
    Catalina State Park, 113–18
Cathedral Rock, 128, 146
Cat Track Tank, 104
Cave Canyon, 216
cell phones, 5
Central Arizona Project (CAP), 21, 53
Chickasaw Indians, 136, 137
Chino Canyon, 205
Chiva Fire, 86, 88
Civilian Conservation Corps (CCC), 31
clothing, 4, 7
cochineal, 87
Coleman, Jeff, 83
Collins, Rick, 83
Columbia Pictures, 16, 57
Copper King Mine, 24, 27–28
copper mining, 16
Coronado National Forest, 102, 176,
    210
Cortés, Hernán, 87
Cowhead Saddle, 84
Cowhead Saddle Trail, 79
creosote bush, 70
cypress, 171

Daniels, Ben, 207
David Yetman Trail, 16, 17, 50–54
daypacks, 4–5
Deer Camp, 99–100
deer dance, 26
dehydration, 708
Desert Mountain Highway, 67
Devil's Peak, 205
difficult trails, 13–14
the Ditch, Tunnel Spring Loop Trail,
    218–19
Dixie Saddle Trail, 125
Doerfer, Joe, 114
Doerfer, Winnie, 114
Douglas Spring Campground, 86, 88, 89
Douglas Spring Trail, 84–89
Dutch John Spring Trail, 195–96

East Fork Trail, 169
easy trails, 14
elegant trogons, 200
Elephant Head, 104
Elephant Head Trail, 204–8
Encinas Trail to Signal Hill, 31–32
Ernie's Falls, 88
erosion
    erosion control, 20–21, 23, 28
    and shortcutting switchbacks, 161,
        163, 179
Esperero Trail, 124–29
Everett, Don, 119–20, 171
extremely difficult trails, 13
Ez-Kim-In-Zin Picnic Area to Signal Hill,
    29–33

False Hope Hill, 106, 107
Father Kino, 101
fees, 2
Fenster School of Arizona, 170
Fenter, Flossie, 210
Fenter, Wert, 210
Finger Rock Canyon, 141
Finger Rock Trail, 133, 137, 141–46, 152
fire
    Aspen Fire, 102, 111
    Chiva Fire, 86, 88
Foster, Lisa, 113

Fuller, James, 103–4
funnel web spiders, 49

Gadsden Purchase, 101, 175, 202
Gardner Canyon
    Kentucky Camp to Gardner Canyon
        Road, 209–14
    and mining, 176
    and Super Trail, 189
    and Tunnel Spring Loop Trail, 216
Garwood Dam, Broadway Trailhead to
    Garwood Dam, 73–77
Garwood, Nelson, 77
Gates Pass, 53, 56
Gates Pass Trail, 52
General Hitchcock Highway, 111, 165
Geronimo Meadow, 128–29
ghost saguaro, 32
Gila monsters, 10
Gilbert Ray Campground, 56, 59
Golden Gate Mountain, 56
Golden Gate Road, 49
Golden Gate Trail, 52
Gordon Hirabayashi Recreation Site
    and Bug Spring Trail, 111
    to Sabino Canyon, 164–69
    to Sabino Canyon Trail, 102
Gould Mine, 16, 35, 37–38
Greaterville, 175, 176
Green Mountain/Bug Spring Trailhead,
    108–9
Green Mountain Trail, 109
Green Valley, 179, 185, 191

hantavirus, 10–11
Happy Valley Campground, 93–94
Happy valley Saddle, 93
hats, 4, 7
Hayden, Carl, 16
Heartbreak Ridge Trail, 93
heat stress and hydration, 7–8
Helen's Dome, 89
Helvetia, 176
Hirabayashi Recreation Site
    and Bug Spring Trail, 111
    to Sabino Canyon, 164–69
    to Sabino Canyon Trail, 102

Hitchcock, Frank Harris, 102, 165
Hohokam people, 15, 26, 31, 33, 65,
    101, 150
homesteading, 16, 54
hoodoos, 109, 111
Hope Camp Trail, 99
Hopkins, Gilbert, 178
Hugh Norris Trail, 16, 17, 18–23, 35
Hummel, Louis, 210
Hutchinson, Roger, 171
Hutch's Pool, 170–74
hydration, 7–8
hypothermia, 11

Ironwood Forest Trail, Cam-Boh–Iron-
    wood Forest–Picture Rocks Wash–
    Ringtail Loop, 60–64
ironwood trees, 62, 63

Japanese-Americans, 111
Javelina Picnic Area, 79
Javelina Wash, 74
Jenko, Carleen, 113
Josephine Canyon, 176
Josephine Saddle
    Agua Caliente (Vault Mine)–
        Josephine Saddle Loop Trail, 199–
        203
    Old Baldy Trail, 180, 182
    Super Trail, 185, 186
Juan Santa Cruz Picnic Area, 59
"jumping cactus," 139
Juniper Basin, 79, 83
Juniper Basin Campground, 82–83

Kennnedy, John, 17
Kent Spring–Bog Springs Loop Trail,
    190–94
Kentucky Camp to Gardner Canyon
    Road, 209–14
Kent, W. H. B., 193
Kimball, Frederick E. A., 146
King Canyon Trail, 24–28, 35
King Canyon trailhead, 22, 23, 38
kit foxes, 32
Kitt Peak, 81, 104, 144, 148, 182, 191,
    192

Lazaroff, David Wentworth, 171
Lead Prospect Mine, 202
Lemmon, Sara Plummer, 101
lightning, 11
Lime Falls, 72
lime kilns, 65, 71–72
Linda Vista Saddle, 143–44
Little Shot Mine, 186
Loma Alta Trailhead, 99
Loma Verde Wash, 74

Madera Canyon, 179, 182
Madera Creek, 200
Maiden Pools, 131, 133
Mam-A-Gah picnic area, 26, 38
Manning Camp, 65–66, 79
Manning Camp Trail, 100
Manning Camp Trail system, 86
Manning, Levi, 65–66
maps, 5
McAneny, George B., 210, 218–19
metates, 156
Mica Mountain, 65
Mile Wide Mining Company, 27–28
Miller Creek Trail, 91, 93
mines
    Copper King Mine, 24, 27–28
    copper mining, 16
    Gould Mine, 16, 35, 37–38
    old mine hazards, 22, 25, 28, 35, 49,
        207
    Rosemont Mine, 176
moderate trails, 14
Montrose Canyon, 160–61
Moreno, Carmen, 72
Mormon Spring, 129
mortar rocks, 133, 150
Mount Hopkins, 180, 182, 185, 186–87
Mount Kimball, 133, 141, 143–44, 146,
    151–52
Mount Lemmon, 67, 101, 111, 120, 152,
    158, 159
Mount Lemmon to Catalina State Park,
    113–18
Mount Wrightson (Old Baldy), 148,
    177–83, 185, 186
movie production, 16

Norris, Hugh, 20
nurse trees, 31–32, 161

Observatory Hill, 71
Old Baldy Trail, 177–83, 200
Old Spanish Trail, 70, 72
Old Tucson Studios, 57
Oury, William, 79
Owen, Billy, 217
Owen, Charles, 217
Owens, Jim, 47

Pack, Arthur, 16
Palisades Canyon, 156
Palisades Trail, 169
Panther Peak, 48
Panther Peak Wash, 45, 47
panthers, 45–47
Peck, A. L., 217
petroglyphs
    King Canyon, 24, 26, 27
    Picture Rocks Wash, 15, 64
    Santa Catalina Mountains, 101
    Signal Hill, 33
Phoneline Trail, 121, 123, 169
Picacho de Diablo, 205
Picacho Peak, 33, 45, 81, 115, 134,
    146
Picture Rocks, 49
Picture Rocks Road, 47
Picture Rocks Wash, Cam-Boh–Iron-
    wood Forest–Picture Rocks Wash–
    Ringtail Loop, 60–64
Pima Canyon Dam, 150
Pima Canyon Spring, 151
Pima Canyon Trail, 144, 147–52
Pima County Board of Supervisors, 50,
    52, 57
Pima people, 15
Pima Saddle, 151
Pink Hill, 77
Pink Hill Trail, Broadway Trailhead to
    Garwood Dam, 73–77
Pontatoc Ridge Trail, 136–40
Pontotoc Mine, 136–37
prickly pears, 87
Prophecy Wash, 49

Pusch Ridge, 146, 150
Pusch Ridge Wilderness Area, 102

Quantrell Mine, 205, 207
Quilter, John "Jake," 99
Quilter Trail, 96–100

ranching, 65, 77, 79, 210
Rancho Romero, 118, 160
Range Rider (Kent), 193
Rattlesnake Canyon, 125
rattlesnakes, 8–9, 125, 127
Rickard, W. T., 104
Rincon Mountains, 65–67
Rincon Peak Trail, 90–95
ringtails, 64
Ringtail Trail, Cam-Boh–Ironwood
　　Forest–Picture Rocks Wash–Ringtail
　　Loop, 60–64
Roadrunner–Panther Peak Wash–Cam-
　　Boh Trail Loop, 44–49
roadrunners, 45
Romero Canyon, 113
Romero Canyon Trail, 102, 115, 118,
　　159–63
Romero, Fabian, 118, 160
Romero Pools, 115, 118, 162, 163
Roosevelt, Theodore, 102, 207
Rosemont Mine, 176

Sabino Basin, 156, 158, 169
Sabino Canyon
　　Blackett's Ridge Trail, 120–23
　　Esperero Trail, 125, 127
　　Gordon Hirabayashi Recreation Site
　　　to Sabino Canyon, 164–69
Sabino Canyon (Lazaroff), 171
Sabino Canyon Trail, 102, 174
Sabino Canyon tram, 154, 158, 165,
　　171
Sabino Creek, 121, 123, 174
saguaro
　　and Agua Caliente Hill Trail, 104
　　and Brown Mountain Trail, 55–56,
　　　58, 59
　　and David Yetman Trail, 53–54
　　and Finger Rock Trail, 145

ghost saguaro, 32
Ironwood Forest Trail, 64
and nurse trees, 31–32, 161
and Quilter Trail, 100
and Sweetwater Trail, 42–43
Saguaro National Park, 16–17, 18, 20–
　　21, 66–67
Santa Catalina Mountains, 21, 45, 101–2
Santa Rita Mountains, 175–76
Santa Rita Water and Mining Company,
　　210
San Xavier del Bac mission, 101
Sawyer Venom Extractor, 9
scorpions, 9–10
Seibold, Frank, 196
Sendero Esperanza Trail, 16, 22, 27,
　　34–38
Sentinel Peak, 15–16
Seri Indians, 62
Seven Falls Trailhead, 122
Shantz, Homer, 66
Shantz Trail, 70, 74
shindaggers, 82, 104, 106, 127, 138, 156
shoes, 4
Signal Hill, Ez-Kim-In-Zin Picnic Area to
　　Signal Hill, 29–33
skin cancer, 6
snakes, 8–9
socks, 4
Southern Arizona School for Boys, 119,
　　170
Spencer Canyon, 154
Sprung Spring, 185
Spud Rock, 89
Squeeze Pen Trail, 77
Stetson, James, 210, 218–19
Stratton, E. O., 101
Summerhaven, 102, 146
Summerhaven Land and Improvement
　　Company, 146
summit sign-ins, 23
sun protection, 6–7
sunscreen, 6–7
Super Trail, 184–89
Sweetwater Trail, 28, 39–43
Sycamore Canyon, 166
Sycamore Dam, 165–66, 168

Sycamore Reservoir Trail, 165–66, 169
sycamores, 133, 191, 192
Sylvester, Art and Anna, 194
Sylvester Spring, 193–94

Tales from Sonoita (Seibold), 196
Tannenbaum, John, 196
Tanque Verde Guest Ranch, 65, 86
Tanque Verde Ridge Trail, 78–83
teddy bear cholla, 139
Temporal Gulch, 176
The Tenderfoot (Kent), 193
Thimble Peak, 122, 154
Three Tank Trail, 88
Tobin, Mitch, 47
Tohono O'odham people, 15, 20, 26, 33,
    82, 101, 182
trail difficulty ratings, 2, 13–14
trailheads and fees, 2
trail registers, 20
Treasure Vault Mine, 202
Tubac, 175
Tucson Citizen, 102, 165
Tucson Mountain Park, 16–17, 53, 54, 55
Tucson Mountains, 15–17
Tucson Prison Camp, 165
Tumacacori mission, 175
Tunnel Spring Loop Trail, 215–19
Tuscson-area hiking
    about, 1–3
    and Africanized bees, 11–12
    and hantavirus, 10–11
    and hypothermia, 11
    and lightning, 11
    readiness, 1, 4–5
    and sun protection, 6–7
trail difficulty ratings, 2, 13–14
trailheads and fees, 2
the Tucson Mountains, 15–17
    and venomous creatures, 8–10
    and water, 7–8
Twin Peaks, 45

ultraviolet index (UVI), 6

Vault Mine, Agua Caliente (Vault Mine)–
    Josephine Saddle Loop Trail, 199–203

venom extraction kits, 9
venomous creatures, 8–10
Ventana Canyon Resort, 131
Ventana Canyon Trail, 129, 130–35

Walker Basin Trail, 217
Walker, William H., 217
walking sticks, 4, 107
Wallace, Henry A., 102
Wasson, John, 20
Wasson Peak, 15, 17, 20, 22, 23, 28, 35,
    41, 42
Watchable Birds of the Southwest
    (Gray), 33
water, 7–8, 25–26
Webber, Frank, 153
West Cactus Forest Drive, 72
Wilderness of Rocks, 114–15
Wild Horse Canyon, 77
Willis, Charles F., 27
Wilson, Link, 136, 137
Wilson, Lutie, 136, 137
the Window, 129, 130, 133–35
Wrightson, William, 178

Yetman, David, 16, 50